salt of the earth

salt of the
earth

 THE NATIONAL TRUST

contents

introduction

Until the Industrial Revolution saw the beginnings of a movement of people from rural areas to rapidly expanding towns and cities, England was largely a land of agricultural communities, deeply rooted in a country life that revolved around the cycle of the farming year.

It was this familiarity with the land, livestock and the natural world that formed the backcloth to much of our superstition, folklore and language. Proverbs and sayings couched in the phraseology of the field and farmyard, the cottage and the country church, became part of everyday speech: a synthesis of wisdom built on generations of experience and observation.

With the shift of people from country to city, many of these turns of phrase lost their immediate rural roots as they widened in usage. Few of us have ever seen a 'bushel', yet we all understand the significance of hiding our 'light' under one. The same holds true of many of the sayings regularly employed as we try to forecast the weather.

The all-important sequence of sowing, tending and harvesting crops has given rise to a sizeable canon of proverbs and sayings; more than a few of which are still followed by farmers and gardeners.

Animals too, whether reared in the field and farmyard, or hunted as game, have inspired an equally influential lexicon of rural lore, of which much is still in current use.

Underlying many of the these time-honoured expressions is a bedrock of traditional beliefs that stem from way back in our history and heritage. This legacy still has us referring to 'the hair of the dog' when we suffer a hangover, making amorous approaches on St Valentine's Day and possibly even avoiding washing blankets in May.

In *Salt of the Earth* traditional sayings that recall elements of country life from times gone by are brought together to reflect changes that have occurred in daily life, while revealing how much turns of phrase we still use owe to our rural forebears.

come ▪
rain
or
shine

When it came to predicting what the weather held in store farming folk and country dwellers in general called on a range of natural 'forecasters': from clouds to cattle, birds to berries, leaves to legends.

Careful scrutiny of apparently unrelated events helped to establish the otherwise incongruous association of cattle swishing their tails with the onset of a thunderstorm, or the crowing of a cock in the evening with rain the following day.

Popular references to mackerel skies, red skies at night and the legend of St Swithin are backed by a substantial body of traditional weather lore which is still valued by many even in an age of satellite imaging and sophisticated meteorological computer modelling.

April weather

Notorious for its 'April showers', the weather in April is seen by many as an indication of what the weather will be like later in the summer.

According to weather lore, thunder in April is generally regarded as beneficial for farmers:

If it thunder on All Fools' Day,
It brings good crops of grass and hay.

When April blows his horn,
'Tis good for hay and corn.

Another saying also finds benefit in a chilly April:

A cold April and a full barn.
or:
A cold April, the barn will fill.

Ash before oak

One of the most widely quoted weather proverbs foretells what the summer will be like from the time that leaves start appearing on two of our native hardwood trees: the ash and the oak. This is known in a number of rhyming versions, of which these are three:

If the oak is in leaf before the ash,
'Twill be dry and warm, and good wheat to thrash;
If the ash be in leaf before the oak
'Twill be cold, and of rain too a great soak.
If the oak and the ash open their leaves together,
Expect a summer of changeable weather.

If the oak is out before the ash
'Twill be a summer of wet and splash;
But if the ash is out before the oak
'Twill be a summer of fire and smoke.

If the oak be out before the ash
There'll only be a little splash;
If the ash be out before the oak
Then there'll be a regular soak.

Barbara and her barns

When a thick band of cloud blankets the western sky with smaller cloud bands above and below it, this is colourfully referred to as:

Barbara and her barns [bairns, children].

This is an obscure reference to St Barbara, who was saved from execution by her own father when he was struck dead by a bolt of lightning just as he was about to chop off his daughter's head. Saved by this unexpected intervention, St Barbara became associated with the power to control thunderstorms and was therefore invoked as a protectress against them.

Bees and weather

Bees have long been respected as accurate weather forecasters. One old rhyme explains:

If the bees stay at home,
Rain will soon come;
If they fly away,
Fine will be the day.

Some farmers who kept bees were in the habit of visiting their hives before deciding on their day's work out of doors. Bees enjoy fine weather, so seeing them out of their hives was a sign that a good day was in prospect:

When the bees crowd out of their hive,
The weather makes it good to be alive.

On the other hand:

When the bees crowd into their hive again,
It is a sign of thunder and of rain.

Candlemas Day

Candlemas Day, 2 February, was traditionally a date of great significance in the country calendar.

In the Christian faith Candlemas is a feast day dedicated to the Purification of the Virgin Mary, but it obviously inherited many old pagan beliefs associated with the Celtic feast of Imbolc which fell the day before, 1 February, in addition to similar festivals celebrated in the Roman world.

Imbolc was a festival that marked the beginning of lambing and the weather in the following weeks was of great importance to shepherds charged with the welfare of new-born lambs and nursing ewes. According to one country rhyme:

As the day lengthens,
So the cold strengthens.

So it is no surprise that Candlemas is the focus of much traditional weather lore.

If Candlemas Day be fair and bright,
Winter will have another flight,
If Candlemas Day be clouds and rain,
Winter be gone and will not come again.

If Candlemas Day be dark and black,
It will carry cold winter away on its back,
But if Candlemas Day be bright and clear,
The half of winter's to come this year.

If Candlemas be fine and clear,
There'll be two winters in the year.

If the birds sing before Candlemas,
They will cry before May.

Where the wind blows on Candlemas Day,
There 'twill abide till the second of May.

These warnings are borne out by the actions of the North American groundhog, which are widely followed in the news media. If a groundhog sees its shadow on 2 February, winter is only half done.

Little wonder then that wise farmers followed the time-honoured precept:

In the barn on Candlemas Day,
Should be half the straw and half the hay.

meaning that half the winter foodstuffs and bedding for livestock should still be stored in readiness.

A variation of this includes the provision of food and fuel for the farmer and his family:

Mary's feast day of the candle;
Half fodder and half fire.

However, the warnings about the continuation of winter were tempered by the milder weather in the West Country, where the arrival of spring has made Candlemas a popular day for sowing beans and peas:

On Candlemas Day if the thorn hangs a drop,
Then you're sure of a good pea crop.

Candlemas Day, put beans in the clay;
Put candles and candlesticks all away.

Cattle forecasting

The behaviour of cattle is a fairly reliable indication of a change in the weather. When rain is on the way, cattle can be seen sniffing the air or shaking their heads. In summer time, cattle sweeping their tails about foretells the coming of a thunderstorm. They do this for a good reason. The prelude to a summer thunderstorm is a warm, humid build-up during which the flies which annoy cattle become particularly active, causing them to swish their tails as they try to rid themselves of the unwanted attention.

Observation of cattle behaving like this has given rise to weather rhymes such as:

When a cow tries to scratch its ear,
It means a shower is very near.
When it clumps its side with its tail,
Look out for thunder, lightning and hail.

Change in the weather

The duration of the warning signs that a period of fine weather is on the change, appears to have some bearing on how long the period of change will last.

The signs of change are familiar in wind, clouds, visibility and temperature. If these changes build gradually, experience shows that the period of bad weather will be longer than if they appear suddenly. This gives rise to the the saying:

Long foretold, long past,
Short notice, soon past.

Christmas weather

Fine weather on Christmas Day is important in ensuring the arrival of a good spring, with few late frosts that could damage delicate fruit blossoms in particular:

If the sun shines on the branches on Christmas Day,
The fruit trees will bear well.

The same appears to be true if Christmas Day is windy:

A windy Christmas Day, a good crop of fruit.

Just to confuse matters are the forecasts that link Christmas sunshine with cold weather to follow in the spring:

If Christmas day be bright and clear
There'll be two winters in that year.

Hours of sun on Christmas Day,
So many frosts in the month of May.

and:

If the sun shines on Christmas Day,
Saddle your horse, and go and buy hay.

By many accounts, the weather to be feared at Christmas is mild weather, since:

A green Christmas means a fat churchyard.

The day of the week on which Christmas falls has its own influence on the weather in the following year, according to a number of sayings, such as:

If Christmas Day falls on a Sunday, the next summer will be
a hot one.
If Christmas Day falls on a Thursday, the following year will
have much wind – and a dry wind that will be.

and:

If Christmas on a Thursday be,
A windy winter you shall see:
Windy days in every week,
Winter weather strong and thick;
Summer shall be good and dry,
Corn and wheat shall multiply.

Cloudy weather

A mackerel sky, the layer of mottled cloud which resembles the colour and patina of a mackerel's skin, is a well-known forerunner of rain, though usually a shower of rain rather than a heavy storm. Many sayings record this:

Mackerel sky – rain is nigh.

A mackerel sky won't last twenty-four hours dry.

Mackerel sky, mackerel sky,
Never long wet, never long dry.

In parts of the country a mackerel sky is known as a 'cruddledy' or curdled sky, and one forecast holds:

Cruddledy sky, cruddledy sky, not long wet, not long dry.

When a mackerel sky is associated with high cirrus clouds, whipped into mares' tails, wind is on the way:

Mackerel sky and mares' tails,
Make tall ships carry low sails.

Some clouds herald fine weather, however. This is particularly true of the fluffy, cotton-wool-like clouds which resemble clumps of wool caught on briars and brambles:

If woolly fleeces strew the heavenly way,
Be sure no rain disturbs the summer day.

The appearance of large cloud masses is a sure sign that rain will not be long in coming:

When clouds appear like rocks and towers,
The earth will be refreshed by frequent showers.

Cock crow at bedtime

Many birds announce the arrival of rain and the farmyard cock is one of the most noticeable. The sound of cocks crowing is usually associated with dawn: however, if they crow in the evening, it foretells the onset of rain:

If the cocks crow when they go to bed,
They'll sure to come down with a watery head.

In other words it will rain the following morning.

Coming of the cuckoo

The cuckoo is the popular herald of spring. The arrival of the 'first cuckoo' is frequently a source of interest in the correspondence columns of national newspapers, although one old saying pegs the dates of its visit to two specific days:

*The cuckoo sings from St Tiburtius' Day (14 April)
to St John's Day (24 June).*

Wise farmers are advised:

*Turn your money when you hear the cuckoo and you'll have
money in your purse till he come again.*

However, if the cuckoo arrives in a late spring, the omens are less favourable. Not only will the trees be bare of leaves, but the spring grass will be late appearing as well, with the result that there will be less fodder for the livestock waiting to be turned out into the fields. A farmer hearing a cuckoo in these circumstances was advised by one rhyme to look to making his profit from his hay rather than his cattle, which would otherwise have eaten it:

*When the cuckoo sings on an empty bough,
Keep your hay and sell your cow.*

In a similar vein farmers were advised:

*When the cuckoo comes to the bare thorn,
Sell your cow and buy your corn.*

Drawing wet

Streaks of light seen radiating from the sun behind a cloud are regarded as a sign of coming rain. They are said to be 'drawing wet' through the action of the 'sun-suckers' sucking up moisture from the earth, to form rain.

Easter perils and promises

The weak condition of cattle in spring, as they recover from the trials of winter, was always a concern:

From Christmas to May
Weak cattle decay.

Easter come soon, or Easter come late,
It's sure to make the old cow quake.

There is some comfort to be had for stockbreeders, however. Animals may not be fat come the spring, but those with a thick coat promise to do well in the summer months ahead:

In spring, hair is worth more than meat.

The weather at Easter was deemed to have its impact on the harvest as well. A wet Easter had this in store:

Rain on Good Friday or Easter Day,
A good crop of hops, but a bad one of hay.

not to mention:

> *If it rains on Easter Day,*
> *There shall be good grass but very bad hay.*

On the other hand, sunshine on Easter Day was welcomed as a sign of good fortune for the summer ahead:

> *If the sun shines on the altar during service on Easter Day,*
> *there will be a good harvest.*

February weather

One way or another February feels a wet month, even if the rainfall is low. Cold weather and a weak sun mean that dampness lingers. Whether rain or snow falls, February ditches invariably fill up, giving rise to the saying:

> *February fill-dyke, black or white.*

February often experiences the coldest temperatures of the year:

> *As the days lengthen,*
> *So the cold strengthens.*

goes a variation of the rhyme and according to another:

> *February makes a bridge [of ice] and March breaks it.*

February as a whole is clearly a month which cannot be relied on when it comes to forecasting the weather. Many a farmer and labourer has had cause to rue the truth of the expression:

A February spring is worth nothing.

If the cat in February lies in the sun, she will creep under the grate in March.

Whereas a wintry February holds the promise of a good summer:

Much February snow a fine summer doth show.

In spite of the fact that February is notorious for floods, whence the expression 'February fill-dyke', statistics show that it can be one of the driest months in the year. Though this may not benefit everyone working the land, according to one proverb:

If in February there be no rain,
'Tis neither good for hay nor grain.

Fine weather dews

If the lawn is dry on a summer morning, experience shows that it will not be long before a shower turns it wet. In contrast, a damp lawn on a summer morning is a welcome sign for those wanting a fine day, as confirmed by the rhyme:

Dew at night,
Next day will be bright.

Flies and rain

When flies settle in large numbers, rain will not be long in coming and one old saying which bears this out is:

If a fly lands on your nose, swat it till it goes,
If the fly then lands again, it will bring back heavy rain.

Football rookies

Football is an ancient pastime with origins far removed from the modern game. It is to the early form of football, a free-for-all in which any number of participants joined in, that the saying 'when the Crows play football', alludes. The reference here is to rooks gathering together in large bodies that circle round each other.

When this happens, rain is on the way.

Forecasting with onions

Onion skin very thin,
Mild winter coming in.
Onion skin thick and tough,
Coming winter cold and rough.

This proverb points to a further benefit of growing one's own vegetables. Presumably imported onions would be of little value in determining the prospects for the coming winter.

Hail to the frost

Late autumn storms of hail foretell the imminent arrival of winter, according to the saying:

A storm of hail brings frost in its tail.

Harvest Moon

The year's moons have traditionally set the pattern to the farming seasons.

In January the frosty mid-winter moon is the farmer's helpmate lighting the frozen fields as the chill night air breaks up the soil in ploughed fields. When spring arrives the moon in April is the germination moon, marking the time for sowing seeds. A month later plants come into leaf with the arrival of the May moon. However, it is the harvest moon that is the most striking and frequently the most significant in the year. This is the full moon that occurs nearest to the autumnal equinox (around 22 September). This bright moon rises for several evenings in a row close to the time that the sun sets. Under these conditions daylight and moonlight join forces in what was once seen as a mark of help from on high in the all-important task of gathering in the crops.

However, the moon was not always a sign of fine harvest weather, as this rhyme shows:

If the moon shows a silver shield,
Be not afraid to reap your field,
But if she rises haloed round,
Soon we'll tread on deluged ground.

I hear thunder

The English summer is often dismissed as 'three hot days and a thunder-storm'. However, thunder in the winter time was regarded as a portent of bad weather later in the farming year which could result in a bad harvest:

Winter thunder, rich man's food, poor man's hunger.

Winter thunder, summer hunger.

Ice in November

Ice in November to walk a duck,
The winter will be all rain and muck.

This saying bears out the warning in others that a cold November can be followed by a mild and, for the farmer, not altogether helpful winter. Little or no frost allows unwelcome pests to survive to cause damage to crops in the following year as well as turning the land waterlogged and heavy, rather than breaking it up with a spell of crisp cold weather.

January weather

January is an unreliable month when it comes to its weather. It can be unseasonably mild or bitterly cold, and if the former there are plenty of sayings to warn against being misled into thinking that spring has arrived early:

A January spring [like a February spring] *is worth nothing.*

If the birds begin to sing in January,
Frosts are on the way.

March in January,
January in March.

If the grass grows in January, it grows the worse for all the year.

For many country people of bygone days, January was a bleak month:

The blackest month of all the year
Is the month of Janiveer.

June weather

June is widely seen as a month of harmonious weather, when nature strikes a balance and appears at ease with herself:

A dripping June
Keeps all things in tune.

goes one saying. Whereas a settled period of weather in June is of benefit to ripening crops:

Calm weather in June,
Sets the corn in tune.

March dust

March is an important month in the fields, when farmers are completing their sowing. Dry, cold weather provides the ideal conditions to finish off this important work, and plenty of dry, windy weather too for good tillage gives ideal conditions, which is why:

A peck of March dust is worth a guinea.

The importance of successful sowing is reinforced by the wise observations:

> *Well sown is half grown.*

and:

> *A dry March never begs its bread.*

Nevertheless, dry weather in March may not be a universal blessing according to the saying:

> *March dust on apple leaf,*
> *Brings all kind of fruit to grief.*

Much of the season of Lent falls in March and has thus given rise to the parallel saying:

> *A dry Lent means a fertile year.*

The wind blowing on the first day of Lent (Ash Wednesday) is also reckoned to set the pattern for the direction of the wind until Easter:

> *Where the wind is on Ash Wednesday,*
> *It will stay all Lent.*

There are warnings about being taken in by the early arrival of spring, which claim that you can never be sure that winter has passed until Lent is over. As one such proverb maintains:

Never come Lent, never come Winter.

The time for sowing is not restricted to March, of course. In parts of the country oats were sown as early as January, if conditions permitted, and the earlier the crop was successfully sown the better the harvest:

Who in January sows oats,
Gets gold and groats:
Who sows in May,
Gets little that way.

As one old saying holds, March is a month of variable weather:

March many weathers.

March is often a month of great contrasts as well, frequently beginning with boisterous, unsettled weather before ending calmly, hence the well-known proverb:

If March comes in like a lion,
It goes out like a lamb.
If it comes in like a lamb,
It goes out like a lion.

The weather in March is also an indicator of what the spring proper may hold in store:

As many mists in March as there are frosts in May.

The direction of the wind on the first day of Spring (21 March and St Benedict's Day), specifically at noon on that day, is regarded as significant in forecasting the wind and weather for several weeks to come:

If the wind is in the east at noon on St Benedict's Day,
It will neither chop nor change till the end of May.

The weather at the end of March is often followed by similar weather at the beginning of April, a phenomenon that gave rise to the proverb:

March borrows three days of April, and they are ill.

May weather

Even though May is ritually associated with the coming of Spring, cold weather in May is often preferred:

A cold May and a windy,
Makes a fat barn and a findy [good weight].
A wet and windy May,
And the barns are full of hay.

A warm and dappledy May,
The barns are full of hay.

Cold May,
Long corn, short hay.

Late April and early May can often be beset by the last blast of winter, when a cold wind sends temperatures falling. Since this frequently co-incides with the flowering of the blackthorn, which turns the hedgerows white with blossom, the cold snap is known as a 'blackthorn winter'.

The same holds true in the warning:

Cast not a clout,
Till May is out.

which cautions against shedding winter clothing too early in the year.

There is some debate whether the 'May' referred to in the rhyme is the month of May, or the hawthorn, which is known by the same name, which also blooms in May.

So, some authorities hold that the proverb warns 'do not begin discarding warm clothing until the hawthorn blossoms', while others maintain that you need to 'wait until the end of May before opening your summer wardrobe'.

However, cold May weather is deemed preferable to warm weather, for one widely held belief maintains that:

A hot May makes a fat churchyard.

Moon and weather lore

According to the time-honoured saying:

The moon and the weather change together.

and scientific investigation in the last fifty years has established what country people have been aware of for thousands of years: that the weather changes with the moon.

One study of the relationship between night-time temperature and the phases of the moon established that there was a regular drop in the minimum night-time temperature for several nights around the time of a full moon.

Similar studies from around the world show the same correlation. One investigation into weather patterns in the USA showed that the phase of the moon could account for nearly 65 per cent of the changes in rainfall, and results of a similar magnitude were demonstrated from a weather survey held in Australia.

As Sir Bernard Lovell, the distinguished astronomer, wrote in the mid-1960s, the links between moon phase and the weather appeared to suggest that 'we are moving through a series of scientific fantasies to a proof of ancient beliefs'.

If the moon shines through a haze, creating 'a watery moon' , rain is on the way. The ring formed round the moon by wet weather was also a good indicator of what lay in store:

Near ring far rain,
Far ring near rain.

Another tell-tale sign of rain, or the lack of it, is the position of the moon, confirmed by the proverb:

Moon on its back, holds water in its lap.

In other words, it brings dry weather. If the points of the moon point downward, the opposite is true and rain is sure to follow.

When the moon shines clear and bright, the following day promises to be fine, and in winter these clear skies warn of frost:

Clear moon – frost soon.

A further guide to the weather is the colour of the moon:

Pale moon does rain,
Red moon does blow,
White moon does neither rain nor snow.

The time of day when the new moon appears is also considered important in assessing the weather for the month ahead:

The nearer to twelve in the afternoon, the drier the moon,
The nearer to twelve in the forenoon, the wetter the moon.

The day of the week carried its own significance, as noted in the saying:

If the moon on a Saturday be new or full,
There always was rain and there always wull.

Bad luck and presumably unfavourable weather too, is said to follow a new moon falling at the beginning of the week:

Sunday's moon comes too soon.

October weather

The weather in October is believed to carry a particular significance for weather well into the New Year, as much as a good six months later:

A warm October presages a cold February.

As the weather is in October, so it will be next March.

Where the wind is at Hollandtide [Hallowe'en], the Season of All Saints, it will be most of the winter.

Of mice and men

There is a common variation of the rhyme which foretells weather later in the winter from the weather in the early part of the season which goes:

If the ice will bear a man before Christmas,
*   it will not bear a mouse afterwards.*

In other words, freezing weather before Christmas is a sign of relatively mild weather to follow in the New Year and for the rest of the winter months.

Pale suns

While a red sky at night is a sign of favourable weather, the opposite is true when the sunset is milky:

If the sun goes pale to bed,
'Twill rain tomorrow it is said.

Plant in the wane of the moon

Sow peasen and beans in the wane of the moon,
Who soweth them sooner he soweth too soone,
That they with the planet may rest and arise,
And flourish with bearing most plentiful wise.

One widely held belief in the farming world was the need to follow the passage of the moon when it came to planting crops.

Thomas Tusser, the Elizabethan farmer who recorded the rhyme above, was noting a common practice by which sowing and planting was undertaken before the new moon. In this way it was hoped that the waxing moon would stimulate the growth of the newly planted crops.

Ploughing with the tide

In coastal districts the movement of the sea brought its own influence to the weather. There are various versions of a popular rhyme which holds that:

> *If it comes on rain when tide's at flow*
> * [coming in and running towards high tide]*
> *You may yoke the plough on any knowe [knoll];*
> *But if it comes when the tide's at ebb,*
> *Then lowse [unhitch] your plough and go to bed.*

Potato birds

One sign of spring welcomed by farmers as an indication that it was safe to begin planting was the arrival of migrant birds, several of which were of significance to particular crops.

In the case of potatoes, the arrival of the wagtail and the cuckoo showed that the time had come to plant the seed crop; indeed the wagtail was nicknamed the 'potato-dropper' and the 'potato-setter'.

In the south-west of England the sound of the first cuckoo called potato farmers to action:

When you hear the cuckoo shout,
'Tis time to plant your tetties out!

Rain before seven

Rain before seven,
Fine before eleven.

is a respected rhyme, which is frequently confirmed by the improvement in the weather that follows a damp start to the day.

Rain from the East

Rain blown by an easterly wind has generally been less welcome than rain falling from the south or west. One saying holds that:

Rain from the East,
Will last three days at least.

An easterly wind is equally unwelcome:

When the wind is in the East,
'Tis neither good for man or beast.

According to a similar rhyme, the same is true for rain driven by a strong wind:

If the rain comes down slanting,
It will be everlasting.

Red skies

Probably the most frequently quoted saying of weather lore is:

Red sky at night, shepherd's delight,
Red sky in the morning, shepherd's warning.

Like many such sayings, there is more to it than rural whimsy and old wives' tales. Indeed, this particular observation draws on biblical authority: when St Matthew describes the occasion when the Pharisees taunted Christ to show them a sign from heaven, he, in reply, told them:

When it is evening, ye say, It will be fair weather:
 for the sky is red.

And in the morning, It will be foul weather today:
 for the sky is red and lowring. O ye hypocrites, ye can
 discern the face of the sky; but can ye not discern the
 signs of the times?

Variations of this include:

> *Evening red and morning grey,*
> *Two good signs for one fine day.*
> *Evening grey and morning red,*
> *Send the shepherd wet to bed.*

and:

> *If the evening be grey and the morning red,*
> *The lamb and the ewe will go wet to bed.*

> *When the reds are out at night it's all the shepherds delight,*
> *But when out in the morning it's all day storming.*

While a red sky might have pleased the shepherd, the appearance of a rainbow came as a mixed blessing to the man working the fields, for:

> *A rainbow at night,*
> *Fair weather in sight.*
> *A rainbow at morn,*
> *Fair weather all gorn.*

However, the first part of this rhyme is contradicted by the notion that:

> *A rainbow at eve,*
> *Sends the ploughboy home with a dripping sleeve.*

The same was also held to be true when the so-called ark appeared in the sky. This was an arch of thin feathery cloud bent across the sky which foretold the arrival of rain:

When the ark is out, rain is about.
When the ark is out,
North and South,
In the rain's mouth.

Seagulls and rain

The sight of seagulls inland has long been taken as a sign of rain, a belief that has given rise to sayings such as:

Seagull, seagull, get thee on't sand,
'Twill never be fine while thou'rt on land.

Snowbones

Patches of snow that stay behind after the rest has melted are known as 'snowbones' and are taken as a sign that more snow is on the way to carry them off.

St Bartholomew

St Bartholomew's Day is 24 August and according to country weather lore, if the weather is settled on this date, there will be a fine autumn:

If St Bartholomew's Day be fair and clear,
Then a prosperous autumn comes that year.

St Swithin

St Swithin's Day (15 July) is perhaps the most significant weather day of the year, for, as the saying goes:

If it rains on St Swithin's Day, there will be rain for forty days.

While there is plenty of evidence to refute this claim, 15 July is still regarded with anxiety by farmers hoping for fine weather for the harvest.

The legend attributed to St Swithin dates from the middle of the ninth century when Swithin, Bishop of Winchester, died. He asked to be buried in the churchyard of the minster, so that the 'sweet rain of heaven might fall upon his grave'. And so he remained peacefully at rest for the next 100 years. When he was canonized, though, it was decided that his body should be moved inside the cathedral to a grave more in keeping with a saint of his standing.

The date set for this transfer was 15 July 971. However, the saint's spirit appears to have been so affronted by the idea that it brought about a downpour of rain which lasted forty days and effectively put an end to any idea of disinterring the former bishop and moving him indoors.

St Swithin's shrine was destroyed during the Reformation, but his reputation and legend live on in sayings like:

> *Oh St Swithin if thou'll be fair,*
> *For forty days shall rain nae mair,*
> *But if St Swithin's thou be wet,*
> *For forty days it raineth yet.*

Summer fogs

Moisture in the air on a summer morning is something to be welcomed, whether it comes in the form of dew, mist or even fog, predictions borne out by sayings such as:

> *Grey mists at dawn,*
> *The day will be warm.*

and:

> *A summer fog is for fair weather.*

Sunshine and showers

> *A sunshiny shower,*
> *Won't last half an a hour.*

is another rhyme that is often proved to be correct, when squalls and brief downpours falling from broken cloud, soon blow away to leave a dry day.

Watching the wise tree

As far back as Roman times, the mulberry tree was a valuable guide in the spring to the passing of frosts and later to their arrival at the close of autumn.

This is due to the fact that the mulberry is probably the most sensitive of our trees. Mulberry leaves do not begin to show until all other trees are bringing forth green buds and even the mildest frost in autumn will set it shedding its leaves.

In the middle of the nineteenth century a clergyman in Huntingdonshire was told by one of his parishioners that 'the wise tree' had not yet begin to bud, '. . . it isn't like some trees as puts out their leaves early and then gets nipped . . .' explained the parishioner. 'You may rest content on the wise tree telling you when you may be safe against frosses.'

Weather according to St Paul

The feast of St Paul falls on 25 January, a date that has traditionally been seen as forecasting the weather for the rest of the year – and not the year's weather alone. If this and similar rhymes are to be believed, St Paul's Day also predicted coming disasters in the months ahead:

St Paul's Day stormy and windy,
Famine in the world and great death of mankind;
St Paul's Day fair and clear,
Plenty of corn and meal in the world.

While this saying takes an entirely optimistic line in claiming:

If St Paul's Day be fair and clear,
Then it betides a happy year.

Weather in the stars

When the stars begin to huddle,
The earth will soon become a puddle.

Free from the glare of street lights, the country sky at night has always been a valuable predictor of what the weather has in store. On some nights there appear to be more stars than there are on others, and the brilliance of the stars themselves seems to vary.

When stars appear to be particularly bright, that is a sign of good weather to come and the fewer stars there are to be seen in the sky the better. Twinkling stars, however, are an indication of windy weather.

On the other hand, those nights when the sky is crowded with stars presage the onset of rain.

The position of the stars in the night sky also marks the movements of the seasons. This is particularly true of the Plough, the easiest formation to pick out, which has long been known as 'Dick and his wagon'. When the handle of the plough is pointing upwards, Dick is said to be taking his wagon up the hill and the weather is likely to be fine. When he is taking his wagon down the hill, the weather is more likely to be wet.

Winter weather

Seasonal weather in its appropriate season has long been taken as a sign that the earth and nature are in harmony, hence the saying:

A good winter brings a good summer.

It is unseasonal weather that forecasts problems ahead and the risk of a poor harvest:

A foot deep of rain,
Will kill hay and grain;
But three feet of snow,
Will make them grow mo'.

Wuthering Heights

Emily Brontë chose the title for her famous novel with an ear for the local turns of phrase used round and about her Yorkshire home at Haworth. Raging, blustering winds which tear across the bleak fells have long been referred to as 'wuthering' over the moors.

the seed-time and the
harvest

Ensuring a successful harvest was more than a matter of profit in centuries past. For most country dwellers it meant the grim difference between a moderately well-fed year and a hungry one.

That distinction may have passed in the developed world today, where refinements in agriculture, storage and transport ensure a ready supply of food throughout the year regardless of seasonal restrictions. Even so, the English language is richly endowed with the wisdom and warnings of husbandry rooted deep in our history.

'Make hay while the sun shines' and 'As you sow, so you reap' are examples of the many turns of phrase still in use which originated long ago in the seasonal changes and working cycle of the agricultural year in which the growth, harvesting and preservation of foods of all sorts was of the utmost importance to the whole community.

All's grist that comes to my mill

Grist is the term used for a quantity of corn to be ground by a miller at any one time. When all the grist is converted to flour, nothing is left over and allowed to go to waste.

Used figuratively, this saying carries the meaning that the speaker can take advantage of anything and is capable of making use of anything or any opportunity presented.

Always room for more

In the days when country parsons still took one tenth of all local produce as their tithe, or tenth part, there was much bad feeling in rural areas when times were hard and harvests poor.

Resentments built up over time and gave rise to sour turns of phrase such as:

Just like the parson's barn.

an expression that was used to describe something that was not so full that it could not take more.

As thin as Banbury cheese

The Oxfordshire market town of Banbury, famous in children's folklore for the nursery rhyme 'Ride a cock-horse to Banbury Cross', is also well-known for Banbury cakes, spiced turnovers that were once a speciality of the town, and Banbury cheese.

The latter is a type of rich milk cheese, which when ready for consumption is about one inch thick, making it considerably slimmer than most English cheeses.

By way of comparison, then, to be 'as thin as Banbury cheese' is to be very thin indeed.

As you sow, so you reap

The image of the sower is drawn upon in a number of instances in Holy Scripture and it is in St Paul's letter to the Galatians that this familiar saying is rooted:

Be not deceived; God is not mocked: for whatsoever a man soweth, that also shall he reap.

For he that soweth to his flesh shall of the flesh reap corruption; but he that soweth to the Spirit shall of the Spirit reap life everlasting.

And let us not be weary in well doing: for in due season we shall reap, if we faint not.

The inference here is clear: the manner of actions has a direct influence on their outcome. In other words, if you conduct yourself well, good will follow from what you do and vice versa.

Bean feast

Bean feasts have always been times of enjoyment. Today's bean feast, an occasional event which marks some significant celebration or annual outing, dates from the time when employers used to treat their employees to a substantial feast at the end of the year.

Beans may well have formed an important part of the menu, though a 'bean goose' is a more likely dish to grace an annual get-together of this sort.

The bean goose, which takes its name from a bean-shaped mark on its bill, arrives in England in the autumn, making it a suitably seasonal addition to a festive occasion a month or two later.

Beans in flower

It was once believed that the scent of bean flowers made people light-headed. Therefore, if the comment was passed of someone that 'the beans are in flower', it was used to explain their silly behaviour.

Blossom time

In the days when cider represented part of a farmworker's wages, the success of the apple harvest was of great significance to farmer and farm-hand alike.

Interest in the apple crop begins at the very start of the year, with the tradition of wassailing orchards on the Eve of Epiphany (Twelfth Night – 5 January). During these festivities toasts are drunk to a chosen apple tree, taking the form of a rhyme or song such as:

Old apple tree, we wassail thee,
And hoping thou wilt bear
For the Lord doth know where we shall be
Till the apples come another year.
For to bear well, and to bear well
So merry let us be.
Let every man take off his hat,
And shout to the old apple tree!
Old apple tree, we wassail thee,
And hoping thou wilt bear
Hatfuls, capfuls, three bushel bagfuls
And a little heap under the stairs
Hip! Hip! Hooray!

From January the period of waiting begins for the first signs of apple blossom, and this too carries its own significance for the outcome of the crop:

If the blossom comes in March,
For apples you may search;
If the blossom comes in April,
You may gather a bag full;
If the blossom comes in May,
You may gather apples every day.

Variations of this theme claim:

When apple trees are in blossom in April and before May
You can put all your barrels away,
But if they blossom at the end of May and the beginning
*   of June*
You can get all your barrels in tune.

and:

If the apple tree blossoms in March,
For barrels of cider you need not sarch;
If the apple tree blossoms in May
You can eat apple dumplings every day.

In other words, the later the blossom the more abundant the apple crop.

No matter how successful a crop may be, tradition holds that we have to wait until the second half of July before picking the crop, as the old saying two pages later reminds us.

Come the autumn, apples are in abundance, although as one old rhyme reminds us, they will remain plentiful for ever:

At Michaelmas [29 September] or a little before,
Half the apple's thrown away with the core.
At Christmas time or a little bit after
If it's as sour as a crab,
It's 'Thank you, master'.

By hook or by crook

In medieval times tenants were granted the right by their lord of the manor to gather firewood 'by hook or by crook'; that is to say by using a shepherd's crook and a billhook. This was a legal entitlement of great value at a time when firewood was the sole means of providing domestic heat.

However, it also imposed restrictions on tenants, since it limited them to taking only wood that could be reached from ground level by the shepherd's crook and cut with the billhook.

The original meaning, of course, implied that taking wood 'by hook or by crook' was a lawful activity. In its modern usage, though, the implication is that anything undertaken 'by hook or by crook' is done either rightfully or wrongly in order to achieve its objective.

Candlemas sowing

The appearance of the sun on Candlemas Day (2 February) is traditionally as unfortunate for farmers as it is for those hoping for an end to winter:

.... 'tis an omen bad, the yeomen say,
If Phoebus shows his face the second day.

If the weather looked favourable and winter was past, 2 February marked an important date in the agricultural calendar:

At Candlemas Day,
'Tis time to sow beans in the clay.

Cherry picking

Since cherries have traditionally been picked by hand, there has always been an element of selection in choosing the ripest and most succulent fruit.

From the country orchard, the expression has passed into modern business life, where 'cherry picking' has become widely used. Following the acquisition of one business interest by another, the dominant partner may be accused of cherry picking if it selects the most profitable sectors of the business and concentrates on maximizing returns from them at the expense of others which perform less well.

Christening the apples

Rain on St Swithin's Day may not be to everyone's approval, but in line with the old saying:

Till St Swithin's day be past,
The apples be not fit to taste.

there is a long-standing belief that without rain to 'christen' them on St Swithin's day (15 July), apples would be worthless.

Conker

The fruit of the common chestnut tree has been known as a conker among children for at least the last two centuries.

The name, conker, may be a corruption of the French word *conque* meaning 'shell', and 'conker' was originally a dialect word for a snail shell, with which an earlier version of the game of conkers was played.

'Conk', the slang word for a nose, may have derived from the same origin; the Duke of Wellington, victor of Waterloo, was known as Old Conky because of his prominent nose.

Corn-showing

It used to be the custom in parts of the country to encourage the wheat crop by a ceremony known as corn-showing, which was performed on the afternoon of Easter Day.

This involved the farm bailiff as well as the farm servants and their families, who gathered in a wheat field with plum cake and cider. A small piece of cake was symbolically buried in the field and a little cider poured over it, before the rest was consumed by the assembled company. When the cake and cider were finished, everyone joined hands and walked across the field repeating:

Every step a reap, every reap a sheaf,
and God send the master a good harvest.

Dogged by St Lawrence

The feast of St Lawrence (10 August) falls within the period known as the 'dog days', which run from 3 July to 11 August. This is often a time of enervating close weather, that saps the energy and puts people in bad moods.

In ancient times it was believed that Sirius, the 'dog star' was responsible for these hottest weeks of the summer, when its heat was combined with that of the sun.

Shakespeare knew all about the malevolent influence of the 'dog days' on human nature: *Romeo and Juliet* is set right in the middle of them and at the beginning of the scene in which two fatal fights take place that change the course of the play, Romeo's friend Benvolio warns the first of the fighters to be killed:

I pray thee, good Mercutio, let's retire.
The day is hot, the Capulets abroad,
And if we meet we shall not escape a brawl;
For now, these hot days, is the mad blood stirring.

Fortunately, the dog-days and 'Lazy Lawrence' tend to make people feel languid and indolent, as expressions such as these indicate:

He've got St Lawrence on the shoulder.

Lazy Lawrence let me goo,
Don't hold me summer and winter too.

Feeling your oats

Common belief maintains that horses are friskier and more energetic after they have eaten oats. Based on this assumption, the saying has been applied over the years to people as well, so that anyone described as 'feeling their oats' can be taken to be behaving in a lively, self-important way, indicative of the fact that they feel well pleased with themselves.

Fertilizing with care

In earlier times, before the arrival of sophisticated agro-chemicals, farmers relied heavily on marl to fertilize their fields.

Marl is a form of loose sedimentary rock or soil made up of clay and lime. However, its use did not ensure universal improvement of the soil, if this saying is to be believed:

If you marl land, you may buy land;
If you marl moss, there is no loss;
If you marl clay, you fling all away.

Franken frosts

Late frosts falling around St Franklin's Day, in the third week in May, can cause serious damage to apples and hops in particular.

These attacks on cider orchards, or hop yards, are blamed on St Franklin, or Franken, who set himself up as a brewer (or cider-maker). In order to ensure good sales, he made a pact with the devil who undertook to attack the blossom from which the rival beverage would be made, in exchange for St Franken's soul. So, in cider-making areas, the devil is said to attack apple blossom, while in those parts of of the country where beer is the principal drink, he attacks young hops.

In both cases the warning is the same beware the Franken nights, and from this has grown the general warning not to put out tender bedding plants until 'after the Franken nights'. For, even if a frost is avoided, these three nights are often unseasonably chilly.

Frying country fish

'I have other fish to fry' is a widely-used and familiar expression meaning 'I am busy at the moment and cannot attend to anything else' and 'I have other things to do'.

However, in time the same sentiment has carried far from the sea into the heart of the countryside, where sayings such as these, couched in farming terms, bear the same meaning:

I have other oats to thresh.
and:
I have another rig to hoe.

A similar transfer of meaning can be seen in a number of country sayings. For example:

To shear [reap] your own rig.

has the same meaning as

'To paddle your own canoe.

Likewise a country dweller who starts something at the wrong end might be said:

To plough the headland before the butts.

The 'headland' is the strip of land left unploughed at either end of a field on which the plough turns. The headlands are only ploughed when ploughing the rest of the field has been completed.

Full of beans

At first 'full of beans' was an expression used to describe a horse that was in first-rate condition and full of energy. The contribution made by beans to the animal's excellent state of health is unclear; as a source of nourishment, beans may have been equated with energy and vitality.

Come the nineteenth century, humans too were benefitting, metaphorically, from the energy-enhancing influence of beans. So anyone deemed to be in 'high spirits' and generally on 'good form' could aptly be described as being 'full of beans' too.

Grasping the nettle

Pulling nettles can be an uncomfortable experience, as anyone who has weeded a garden over-run with nettles will tell you. However, nettles are less likely to sting a bare hand if they are held tightly rather than tentatively.

Hence the countryman's wise advice to grasp nettles tightly, to avoid being stung by them, as the poet Aaron Hill commented in the first half of the eighteenth century:

> *Tender-handed stroke a nettle*
> *And it stings you for your pains;*
> *Grasp it like a man of mettle,*
> *And it soft as silk remains.*

This is carried into the metaphorical sense of the saying when it is used as an encouragement to face difficulties firmly and to tackle situations boldly.

Here we go gathering nuts in May

Since no nuts have formed by the time May arrives, none can be gathered, which appears to render as nonsense this old country rhyme, made popular by children. However, if a couple of minor changes are made, the rhyme does indeed make sense.

'Here we go gathering nuts in May' is an example of how words in traditional rhymes have sometimes become confused with other words with similar sounds. In this case, the original rhyme ran 'Here we go gathering knots of May', which referred to the long-held practice of gathering knots of flowers on May Day.

Hiding your light under a bushel

In times gone by grain and other dry goods were measured in a wooden or earthenware container, holding, and therefore known as, a 'bushel'.

Self-evidently, anything placed under the upturned bushel would be hidden from sight. So those who were modest and self-effacing about their abilities were described as hiding their light 'under a bushel', where their talents remained hidden from the sight of others.

Horse chestnut

At one time the fruit of the common chestnut tree (better known as the conker, described earlier) was used as a medicament for horses. A herbal written at the end of the sixteenth century confirms this:

> *For that the people of the East countries do with the fruit thereof cure their horses of the cough . . . and such like diseases.*

So it was only natural that the tree producing the fruit should in time become associated with horses as well, hence the name horse chestnut.

Another explanation links the leaf-stalk of the horse chestnut with a horse's anatomy. When a leaf-stalk is removed, it looks very like a miniature horse's hock and foot with shoe and nail marks.

I don't care a fig for you

The fig was not a feature of the English rural diet, or its husbandry, in days gone by.

So, it presents an apparent problem with this popular term, until we realize that the 'fig' referred to is not the tasty fruit of the fig tree, but the 'figo' or 'fico' (also known as the 'Spanish fig'), which was a common gesture of contempt, made with the thumb and fingers which was well known in the England of Shakespeare's day. In *Henry V* Shakespeare offers this definition in the hot-headed exchange between Pistol and Fluellen:

> Pistol: *Die and be damn'd! and figo for thy friendship!*
> Fluellen: *Its well.*
> Pistol: *The fig of Spain!*

'I don't care a fig for you' and similar turns of phrase, such as 'I don't give a fig' carry the same unmistakable meaning as snapping one's fingers at someone while declaring 'I don't care that for you'.

In meal or in malt

Millers were invariably regarded with suspicion by their neighbours, since many were convinced that the miller regularly took more than his fair share of the harvest as it passed through his hands.

This underlying doubt about a miller's conduct gave rise to the saying 'in meal or in malt', both of which were end products of the grain milled by the miller.

Since both meal and malt had the potential to produce a profit, and since the miller was entitled to a share of the proceeds as his payment, he would benefit whatever the milled grain was used for.

'In meal or in malt' then is a figurative rendering of 'in one way or the other', or 'directly or indirectly'.

In the morning sow thy seed

The movement of the sun is said to have an effect on plant growth. Where circumstances allowed, farmers tried to sow corn and similar crops in the morning, while the sun was still rising towards noon.

Root crops, potatoes and the like, which grow below ground, were reckoned to prefer afternoon sowing, so that they could 'sink down' with the sun.

The same distinction was drawn when grass was mown: cutting grass in the morning was believed to promote growth, whereas cutting grass in the afternoon was supposed to have the opposite effect.

Knowing how many beans make five

Anyone who knows 'how many beans make five' is no fool. More to the point, he or she is not to be put upon.

The reference is to a traditional catch: How many beans make five? The answer, self-evidently, is five.

Then comes the supplementary question: But how many blue beans make five white beans?

The correct answer is: Five – when they have been peeled.

That's the significance of 'knowing how many beans make five'.

Looking for a needle in a bottle of hay

This saying from the hay field has the same meaning as the more familiar 'looking for a needle in a haystack', but brings a degree of confusion in its use of the word 'bottle'.

Bottles, of course, are generally used to contain fluids; hay, on the other hand, is collected into huge bundles, variously known as bales or ricks. And here is a not unfamiliar example in English of two words with quite separate meanings sharing the same spelling.

By the fourteenth century 'bottle' was established in English as the anglicized form of the old French word *botel*, the diminutive of *botte*, meaning 'a bundle'.

With this in mind, it is easy to see that 'looking for a needle in a bottle of hay', actually means 'looking for a needle in a small bundle [bale] of hay'.

Luck with the rooks

The presence of rooks was always regarded as a sign of prosperity. Farmers used to encourage rooks to nest in their trees, working on the belief that:

Rooks only build where there's money.

Some even went to the extent of building artificial nests in the hope that these would attract the luck-bringing birds to their land.

Make hay while the sun shines

Although very few of us make hay today, we know the value of taking advantage of an opportunity; or striking while the iron is hot, to draw an analogy with the blacksmith's shop.

Before the days of mechanical cutting, tedding and baling, fine weather was essential to ensure a satisfactory crop of hay. Today a wet spell during haymaking can cause difficulties for even the best equipped farmer.

Mixing your drinks

Haymaking and harvesting in hot summer weather was dry, dusty work, especially when it was done by hand. Considerable quantities of cider were consumed by workers in the field as they toiled under relentless summer skies.

In many country areas cider provided their fluid intake, but mixing cider with beer could lead to problems, if the following rhyme was not carefully observed:

Cider on beer
Is very good cheer.
Beer upon cider
Makes a bad rider.

Moon fruit

The Romans believed that fruit picked when the moon was waning had the best flavour, and a waning moon has always been favoured when it comes to harvesting apples.

As one old piece of advice holds:

The moone in the wane,
Gather fruit for to last.

This was confirmed by a Victorian writer who observed:

It is a very common custom among the farmers and
peasantry of Devonshire to gather in the 'hoard fruit' in
the 'shrinking of the moon . . .' apples then bruised in the
gathering-in, do not decay afterwards.

Noon sowing

In 1805 the *Old Farmer's Almanac* echoed the widely held belief:

Set cabbages in the middle of the day.

More than two and a half centuries later scientific research suggested that there might be a natural incentive for following this advice. Experiments conducted with a variety of plants showed that they followed a daily rhythm in which sap rose in the morning until midday, when the plants appeared to reach a stasis in which they effectively 'marked time'. As afternoon wore on and sunlight declined, activity in the plants was reduced and as evening settled, they appeared to be more firmly rooted to the soil than had been the case in the morning.

Not worth a row of beans
The humble bean, nutritious and serviceable as it may be, has seldom been held in high esteem and it certainly is not regarded as being of significant value in this saying.

Describing someone or something as not being 'worth a row of beans' places that individual or object at a very low value indeed, even taking into consideration the fact that individual beans are planted in a row to produce a full crop when they ripen.

Not worth a rush
When the floors of homes were made of beaten earth, the only floor covering consisted of rushes strewn over the floor. The strewing of clean rushes was reserved for visitors of distinction and status. Those who did not reach that standing in the eyes of the householder had to make do with used rushes or nor rushes at all. Therefore to be considered 'not worth a rush' amounted to being regarded as having little significance and from this 'not worth a rush' acquired its broader meaning of being worthless.

On the nail

The nail referred to in this saying from the medieval market place, resembles the shape of a carpenter's nail, though it is a great deal bigger.

The nail in the market was a stand topped by a shallow vessel which formed the focal point for market trading. Vendors would place of samples of their goods, frequently grain, in the vessel where they would be inspected by potential purchasers. If the purchasers were satisfied with the quality and price of what was being offered to them, they would seal the bargain by placing their payment in the vessel as well; in other words paying 'on the nail'.

From medieval markets use of the term widened to the point where paying 'on the nail' implies immediate payment for goods or services.

Out of the parsley bed

At one time parsley was believed to be an aphrodisiac and until the twentieth century a 'love child' was often described as being 'out of the parsley bed'.

Pay-rent

The payment of rents for many agricultural tenancies have traditionally fallen due on the four quarter days of the year: Lady Day (25 March), Midsummer Day (24 June), Michaelmas Day (29 September) and Christmas Day (25 December).

Prompt payment of rent was a confirmation of success in the preceding months and 'pay-rent' became a well-used synonym for 'profitable', in sayings like:

A proper pay-rent sort o' pigs.

and:

A rare pay-rent piece o' beans.

Peppercorn rents

Peppercorn rents have been established in English property law since the Middle Ages. Even at that time a single peppercorn was of very little value, but the practice of paying even this nominal rent was evidence enough in the eyes of the law that a rent had been paid and that the contract between landlord and tenant had been fulfilled.

Peppercorn rents enabled tenants to enjoy virtually free ownership of their land and other rented property, while allowing the legal owner to retain the ultimate rights to the freehold.

Planting by the Bible

In the traditional table of church readings, Genesis is started on the third Sunday before Lent, which is usually in the first or second week of February and is finished by about the second week in March.

Away from church, this was a time when country gardeners were busy preparing for crops later in the year. According to one old saying:

> *By the time Genesis is finished, your garden should be planted.*

Plough Monday

Plough Monday, the first Monday after the Twelfth Day of Christmas, marked the end of Yuletide celebrations and a return to the fields in country districts.

There was a time when maid servants all over England competed with others in the household to see who would be the first to be out of bed and busy on that first day when the normal routine of work began again.

The same was true of farmers and their farm servants when they returned to the fields, encouraged by sayings like:

Plough deep, while sluggards sleep;
And you shall have corn to sell and keep.

Ploughman's lunch

While it is more than likely that a midday meal comprising bread, cheese and pickle may have sustained ploughmen and other farm labourers in the fields for centuries, the term 'ploughman's lunch' is comparatively recent.

The phrase was coined in the 1970s by the English County Cheese Council, who used it as an advertising slogan. It certainly sounded suitably rustic and melded with the image of 'Olde England' fostered by many public houses, where it was soon a widely promoted item on the menu, later to be abbreviated to the otherwise incongruous name 'ploughman's'.

Planting with the leaves

The arrival and growth of leaves with the coming of spring was watched with particular interest by farmers and country gardeners. Particular trees gave guidance for particular crops. So the leaves on elm trees acted as useful indicators for kidney beans:

When elmen leaves are as big as a shilling,
Plant kidney beans if to plant 'em you're willing.
When elmen leaves are as big as a farden,
Plant kidney beans in your garden.
When elmen leaves are as big as a penny,
Plant kidney beans if you mean to have any.

The success of a barley crop was also linked in popular country belief to the appearance of leaves, as this saying confirms:

When the elm leaf is as big as a mouse's ear,
Then to sow barley, never fear.

Pulling the chestnuts out of the fire

Since the Middle Ages 'pulling the chestnuts out of the fire' has been used in the sense of retrieving a difficult situation for someone, often by extricating them from an embarrassment.

The allusion in the saying is to the old fable of the monkey and the cat. The monkey discovers chestnuts roasting in the embers of a fire and decides he would like to eat them. However, removing the chestnuts from the fire would risk burning his paws, so the monkey persuades his friend the cat to use his paws to pull the chestnuts from the fire for him.

Put out the miller's eye

This is another critical saying employing the miller, though this time the miller is not the subject of censure. That is reserved for the cook who prepares a broth or pudding so thin that even the keen eye of a miller would be hard put to detect the flour in it.

Salt of the earth

Salt was a vital commodity in the ancient world. Roman soldiers received part of their pay as a *salarium*, an allowance with which they bought salt; the English word 'salary' is derived from this.

Salt was used to preserve food as well as season it, and the saying 'salt of the earth' received its ultimate endorsement when Christ used the term to describe his disciples in the Sermon on the Mount:

> *Ye are the salt of the earth: but if the salt have lost his savour, wherewith shall it be salted? It is thenceforth good for nothing, but to be cast out, and to be trodden under the foot of men.*

From this point on, anyone described as the salt of the earth could reasonably regard themselves as among the best of mankind.

Settling on the lees

Lees occur in wine making as a sediment which collects at the bottom of a barrel or bottle. These are the dregs that are thrown away after the wine has been removed.

Anyone obliged to settle on the lees, is forced to resort to settling down on what is left after the best has gone, in other words to making do with what is left after the main part of one's resources have been consumed, often recklessly.

Shearing time

Care needed to be taken when it came to shearing sheep. As this rhyme suggests, shearing sheep at the wrong time of the year could have serious consequences:

Shear your sheep in May,
And shear them all away.

Sloes and barley

Sloe is another term for the blackthorn, best known for its small bluish-black fruit, with a sharp sour taste, from which the warming winter liqueur, sloe gin, is made.

Covered in blossom, the blackthorn is a mass of delicate white flowers, one of the heartening signs of spring after the dull months of winter.

The arrival of blackthorn blossom was also a valuable sign for farmers, following the time-honoured advice:

When the slae [sloe] tree is white as a sheet,
Sow your barley, whether it be dry or weet.

Small potatoes

Although the potato arrived in England comparatively recently (500 years ago or thereabouts) it did not take long to become rooted in the language in several turns of phrase of which 'thinking small potatoes' was one of the first.

'Small potatoes' (originally 'little potatoes') came to mean something of little consequence and to 'think small potatoes' of something implied that it was of very little significance.

Sowing wild oats

In agricultural terms wild oats are weeds: poor quality cereals as opposed to the richer yielding crop of cultivated oats. On some farms wild oats have been hand-weeded from fields of growing corn well into modern times.

To sow wild oats, then, is to undertake a reckless and frankly wasteful course of action and it has long been used with reference to young people (invariably young men) who 'sow wild oats' by indulging in the final excesses of youth before they settle down to lead mature and profitable lives.

Sowing and the Grim Reaper

In days gone by, sowing seed had important symbolic as well as practical implications. According to one long-held belief, missing seeding a row in a field would lead to the death of a relative, an anxiety which gave rise to the saying:

Mustn't miss a row, or we'll lose one of the family.

Sowing with the saints

The first three weeks in March are traditionally times for sowing peas and beans. In the church's year these equate to the period between the feast days of St David and St Chad (1 and 2 March) and that of St Benedict (21 March).

As this rhyme shows, farmers who missed sowing by the feast of St Benedict were advised not to sow at all that year:

Sow beans or peas on David and Chad,
Be the weather good or bad;
Then comes Benedict,
If you ain't sown your beans –
Keep 'em in the rick.

Taking pot luck

When most household cooking took place over an open fire the majority of meals were prepared in a large cooking pot that was kept boiling over the fire. This contained everything that was to be consumed in the meal: vegetables, cereals and, on occasion, a small amount of meat. With catering of this sort, a meal from the pot comprised whatever had been put into the pot to cook and 'taking pot luck' amounted to offering visitors the opportunity to join the family meal and share whatever happened to be in the pot at that time.

This was in contrast to preparing a special meal for visitors in advance and 'taking pot luck' retains its original meaning even though cooking pots have been replaced by modern domestic cookers and microwaves. Anyone invited to 'take pot luck' shares in whatever the family is going to eat, without any special provision for visitors.

The Devil's offering

When it came to seed-sowing, it was always considered to be important to make a contribution to the devil to ensure good crops. Indeed when seeds were dropped into the soil rhymes such as this were once common; although whether the farmer or a more sinister 'Master' was the beneficiary is uncertain:

Four seeds in a hole
One for the birds
One for the mice
And one for the Master.

In the same way sowers working in the fields would offer a token offering of seed, using words such as:

This is for me,
This is for my neighbour,
This is for the Devil.

and:

One to rot and one to grow,
One for the pigeon, one for the crow.

The mill cannot grind with the water that is past

This old proverb dates from a time when watermills ground much of the flour in England. Once water had flowed past the mill, it could not be brought back to turn the mill a second time. The implication of the saying, self-evidently, is that you need to seize opportunities when they are presented, because once they have moved beyond you they cannot be retrieved.

The moon and mushrooms

The moon was believed to exercise its influence over field mushrooms, which should only be picked, if tradition is to be believed, when the moon is waxing:

When the moon is in the full, mushrooms you may freely pull,
But when the moon is on the wane, wait ere you think to
pluck again.

The rotten apple injures its neighbour

At the heart of this and similar proverbs and sayings involving rotten apples is the fact that allowing apples to come into contact with each other risks letting the disease in a rotten apple spread to others.

This is why traditional wooden apple racks are arranged to ensure that apples can be stored on wooden slats, with a safe distance between each one. If an apple does become rotten, it will remain isolated from the others and the rest of the crop will remain free of infection.

When it is used metaphorically, 'a rotten apple' is the term applied to an individual whose presence and influence has a deleterious effect on others, especially anyone who comes into close contact with him or her.

The wisdom of Thomas Tusser

Thomas Tusser was an agricultural writer and poet who lived in the middle of the sixteenth century. In 1557 he published his *Hundred Goode Pointes of Husbandrie*, which remained a well-thumbed and hugely popular handbook on farming for generations to come. So influential was Tusser's work that many proverbs can be traced back to his writing.

Tusser chose to impart his words of wisdom in a series of succinct and, most importantly, easily memorable rhymes. For example he offered these nuggets of advice during the farming year:

> *By sowing in wet*
> *is little to get.*

from *Marches abstract*.

> *Get into the hopyard, for now it is time,*
> *to teach Robin hop on his pole how to climb.*

from *Maies husbandrie*.

> *The better the muck*
> *the better good luck.*

from *Works after harvest.*

> *Good dwelling give bee*
> *or hence goes shee.*

from *Septembers abstract.*

> *Keepe [scare away] crowes, good sonne,*
> *see fencing be done.*

from *Octobers abstract.*

> *When frost will not suffer to dike and to hedge,*
> *then get thee a heat with thy beetle and wedge.*

> *[in other words split wood when you can't mend fences and*
> *hedges]*

from *Decembers husbandrie.*

Thistle cutting

Weeds grow as well as crops in the warm soils of spring, however the temptation to cut them too early had to be avoided if they were to be dealt with satisfactorily. The following rhyme helps to drive the point home:

Cut thistles in May,
They grow in a day.
Cut them in June,
That is too soon.
Cut them in July,
They will surely die.

Time and motion study

Before the mechanization of most agricultural work, productivity on a farm depended on the efficient use of manpower. This no doubt gave rise to the wry old farmer's saying:

One boy is a boy,
Two boys is half a boy,
And three boys is no boy at all.

Thomas Tusser advised proper rewards for honest workers and keeping a keen eye for shirkers, especially at harvest time.

In some parts of the country the principal reaper was known as the harvest lord. It was his task to work first in a row, setting the rate for the rest of the reaping team:

Grant harvest lord more by a penie or twoo,
to call on his fellowes the better to doo:
Give gloves to thy reapers, a larges to crie,
and dailie to loiterers have a good eie.

from *Augusts husbandrie*

Once the harvest was gathered and safely stored it was time for the tradi-tional harvest celebration, when farmers and farm servants celebrated another (hopefully) successful year. Here is Thomas Tusser again:

In harvest time, harvest folke, servants and all,
should make all together good cheere in the hall;
And fill out the black boule of beith to their song,
And let them be merie all harvest time long.

Once ended they harvest, let none be begilde,
please [pay] such as did helpe thee, man, woman,
and childe.
Thus dooing, with alway such helpe as they can,
thou winnest the praise of the labouring man.

from *Augusts husbandrie*

Up corn, down horn

This is an old saying which points to the relative prices paid for corn and beef ('horn') at markets in days gone by. When corn prices were high, the price of beef tended to fall, since buyers had less money to spend on meat.

Wassail toasts

In parts of the country it was customary to toast the animals (and by association the farm as a whole) on Twelfth Night. Custom dictated that the farmer and his farm servants would visit the oxen in their stalls, raising a toast to each one, calling each by name while reciting:

Here's to thee benbow, and to thy white horn,
God send thy master a good crop of corn;
Oh wheat, rye and barley, and all sorts of grain;
You eat your oats, I'll drink my beer,
May the Lord send us a happy new year.

When each ox had been toasted, a specially baked plum cake with a hole in the centre was placed over a horn of the first ox, which was then encouraged to shake his head and send the cake flying one way or the other; if it fell in one direction, the farmer had the cake, in the other and it went to the farm servants.

Sometimes the toast was offered by the farmer's wife, who might say:

Fill your cups my merry men all,
For here's the best ox in the stall,
Oh, he is the best ox, of that there's no mistake,
And so let us crown him with the Twelfth cake.

If the plum cake was placed on the horn of a heifer, this form of toast was used:

Here's health to the heifer,
And to the white teat,
Wishing the Mistress a house full of meat.
With cruds [curds], milk and butter, fresh every day,
And God grant the young men keep out'n her way.

Weeding by the solstice

Traditional belief holds that pulling weeds before the summer solstice, after which the days shorten, is ineffectual. Successful weeding, so the thinking goes, can only be undertaken once the year begins its gradual decline from mid-summer:

Who weeds in May
Throws all away!

Working up to the collar

This expression comes from the time when horses provided the principal drawing power on and off the road.

Draught horses were fitted with heavy horse collars to which were attached the chains or shafts of the plough or vehicle they were pulling. If a horse was 'working up to the collar', in other words pulling so hard that the collar was fixed firmly round its neck and shoulders, it was pulling well, using great effort. By contrast horses that let their collars hang loose round their necks were not putting in the same amount of effort.

From horses, the saying has transferred to people. Those 'working up to the collar' are deemed to be working with real effort, avoiding any temptation to take things easy.

all god's
creatures

Familiar sayings such as 'the black sheep of the family', 'dyed in the wool' and 'the pecking order' echo aspects of country life and work which were once commonplace. When the production of wool and cloth was a key component of the national economy, albeit operating at the level of a cottage industry in many places, the simple technology of wool dyeing would have been widely understood. In the same way, the hierarchy which ruled the fowl ranging free in a farmyard would have been familiar to everyone who kept even a few chickens.

Modern methods of livestock rearing and food production, coupled with population concentrations in and around urban areas, may have divorced us from day-to-day contact with most creatures other than our domestic pets, yet many sayings concerning animals and birds of all descriptions remain ingrained in the language we hear, use and read.

All his geese are swans

There are echoes of the tale of the Ugly Duckling in this saying, although it does not convey the happy ending of the nursery story.

The swan was, and remains, a royal bird both on the water and on the table. Only those of the highest station had leave to dine on swan; while geese were popularly consumed by one and all.

'All his geese are swans' has two related meanings, both of which point to over-inflated opinions on the part of those who see the world through rose-tinted glasses. 'All his geese are swans' could be ascribed to anyone who overestimates; the same is true of the man whose children are paragons in his own eyes and who remains firmly convinced that everything he does is superlative.

The saying is also used in its reverse form: 'All your swans are geese'. This is the inevitable retort when fine promises or boastful expectations are proved to be ill-founded.

As a pig loves marjoram

Ever since pigs were first kept as domestic animals it has been clear that they have a deep aversion to all of the aromatic plants belonging to the marjoram family.

Since pigs have this deep loathing for marjoram, the saying 'as a pig loves marjoram' is an ironic and emphatic way of saying 'not at all'.

As the crow flies

Traditionally crows have been believed to fly back to their nests using the most direct line of flight and the saying became popular from the early nineteenth century, when a greater mobility began in society, as an indication of the shortest distance between two points.

Strictly speaking, it is the rook rather than the carrion crow which flies in a direct line back to its nest, though country people have been less concerned with the crow's 'flight path' than with its altitude. High-flying crows, returning in the evening to their nests, have long been regarded as a portent of fine weather the following day, whereas crows taking a low-level route home in the evening suggest that the next day will be wet.

As well be hanged for a sheep as a lamb

It was only in the nineteenth century that the theft of a sheep or a lamb in some parts of the country ceased to be punishable by death.

Two centuries earlier the saying 'as well be hanged for a sheep as a lamb' was already a much-quoted proverb, implying that if the consequences are the same, it is worthwhile aiming for something of higher value than of lower.

As it developed, the saying broadened in meaning, advising against stopping at half-measures, but encouraging boldness of endeavour, particularly when an illicit enterprise was being undertaken.

At the end of your tether

Most of us at some time have experienced the intense exasperation which comes when our patience and self-control reach their limit and we get to the point of total despair and utter frustration, which, to put it another way, leaves us at 'the end of our tether'.

The analogy in this well-used turn of phrase is to an animal left to graze, but secured by a rope, or tether, rather than being allowed to roam freely. Such an animal can graze as far as its tether will let it move from the point where the tether is secured. Once it reaches the end of the tether, it cannot move further. Fettered like this, the grazing animal might perhaps experience the frustration which has given rise to the expression.

Bacon brains

For hundreds of years the only meat available to English peasants was bacon, unlike those of higher social standing who had access to finer cuts of meat, such as beef and venison. Bacon became associated with the peasantry and in time 'bacon brains' became synonymous with referring to someone as a 'simpleton', or a slow-witted yokel.

Bald as a coot

The coot is water bird with black plumage which contrasts sharply with its white bill that extends up to its forehead. This striking appearance makes it look at a glance as if it is bald and people with hairless heads have been referred to as being 'as bald as a coot' from as long ago as the thirteenth century.

Beating about the bush

The hunt, the chase and latterly the shoot have been features of rural life since ancient times and it is from these that the saying 'beating about the bush' comes.

In the sporting field, game of all sorts takes refuge in thickets. Huntsmen in pursuit of game, whether using dogs, nets, bows and arrows, or shotguns, always employ great caution in approaching undergrowth or dense woodland where their quarry may be hiding.

When the hunters are in place and ready, teams of beaters surround the 'bush' and then move through it systematically, driving the game towards the waiting hunters. From this, the saying 'beating about the bush' has adopted a wider meaning in which it is applied to approaching a subject cautiously and in a roundabout way, as opposed to tackling it head on.

Beware the magpie

The magpie has always been regarded as an ominous bird. When a single magpie is seen, that is invariably taken as a sign of evil; however, the significance of seeing two or more varies around the country, as these versions of the familiar rhyme show:

One for sorrow
Two for mirth
Three for a wedding
Four for a birth.

Yan is sorrow
Twea is mirth
Three is weddin'
Fower is birth
Five is silver
Six is gold
Sebben is a secret, niver to be told.

Yen's sorry
Twee's morry
Three's a wedding
Fower's deeth
Five's hivin'
Six is hell
And Sivin's the deel aan sel.

One, sign of anger
Two, sign o' muth
Dress, sign o' wedding-day
Vower, sign o' death
Vive, sign o' zorrow
Zix, sign o' joy
Zebm, sign o' maid
An eight, sign o' boy.

Black sheep

From the time when the wool trade became established as the backbone of the English economy in the Middle Ages, black sheep were considered less valuable than white ones, because their wool could not be easily dyed.

Since most domestic sheep range in colour from white to light brown, black sheep have always been in the minority. By the eighteenth century, a 'black sheep' had come to mean a person out of favour; someone oddly different and therefore a renegade.

The idea of the 'odd one out' in a flock is still current when the least successful or admirable member of a family is referred to as 'the black sheep of the family'.

Bringing home the bacon

For centuries pigs were awarded as prizes at country festivities. Bowling for a pig or catching a greased pig were popular rural pastimes enjoyed on feast days and other holidays. Pigs were significant prizes as well, representing as they did the only source of meat for many families.

Those who were successful in winning a pig, literally brought home the bacon and 'bringing home the bacon' became a well-used euphemism for winning a prize or succeeding in some form of contest.

Chewing the cud

Among human beings, 'chewing the cud' describes a reflective state of mind in which people think deeply about something, especially the past.

The saying is a figurative borrowing, of course, referring to the digestive process of animals such as cattle, which are able to regurgitate food in order to chew it in their mouths again. Cattle in particular have a ruminative look about them while they chew the cud and the adjective 'ruminative' of course derives from the noun 'ruminant', the name given to animals which chew the cud; both English words stem from the Latin verb *ruminare*, which means 'to chew over again'.

Cock of the walk

The area of a farmyard where poultry used to be fed was known as the 'walk' and if there was more than one cock in residence they would fight it out to achieve supremacy of this all-important patch of ground. The victor, inevitably became 'cock of the walk' and from farmyard poultry the term acquired its figurative use in describing any domineering individual.

Cock-a-hoop

Since the sixteenth century cock-a-hoop has meant jubilant or exultant, although its origins remain a matter of some dispute.

Some maintain that the term describes the process of removing the 'cock' or spigot from a barrel of beer and laying it on the hoop, allowing the beer (and subsequent good cheer) to flow freely.

Another explanation looks to the farmyard cock, whose triumphant crowing conveys its own sense of jubilation.

Cooking your goose

Geese were traditionally eaten at Michaelmas when autumn was well under way and winter fast approaching. Before the development of ways of storing and preserving food safely, this would have been the start of a long period during which whatever food was available would become increasingly scarce and less palatable. Cooking and eating the goose for many people represented the last taste of fresh meat for many months and this may have given rise to the metaphorical sense in which the saying is now used. For 'cooking your goose' means ruining your chances, or making a disastrous mistake; while 'cooking someone else's goose' means ruining their plans.

Don't count your chickens before they are hatched

The origin of this well-known proverb lies in one of Aesop's fables which tells the tale of a dairy maid so preoccupied with the eggs she was going to buy with the proceeds from the sale of her milk, that she lost concentration and allowed the pail to fall over, losing all her milk in the process.

From this cautionary tale, the saying 'Don't count your chickens before they are hatched' has become a well-established warning not to make, or act on, an assumption which turns out to be wrong, even if the prospects appear to be favourable.

Don't look a gift horse in the mouth

This saying has a similar to 'Straight from the horse's mouth' and both allude to the common practice of examining a horse's front teeth to establish its age.

'Don't look a gift horse in the mouth' warns the recipient of a present against enquiring too closely into its intrinsic value. The advice at the root of the expression is, be happy to have received the gift and leave it at that.

Dyed in the wool

'Dyed in the wool' dates from the time when the wool trade and associated cloth industry in England was well established and serving a growing market at home and on the Continent.

Cloth that was made from wool which had been dyed before weaving, in other words dyed in the wool, kept its colour for much longer than cloth that had been dyed after weaving.

From this practical example of durability and reliability stemmed the wider use of the phrase which came to mean 'thorough-going' and 'one hundred per cent' – the anithesis of short-lived and superficial.

Eating Dunmow bacon

As far back as the year 1111 a custom was established in Dunmow in Essex which rewarded successful applicants with a side of bacon, or a flitch as it is also known.

The applicants, all of whom had to be married men, had to present themselves at the door of the church in Dunmow, where they were required to kneel on two sharp stones while swearing that for twelve months and a day they had never had a disagreement with their wives or wished themselves unmarried.

Although the custom fell from use on occasions, it was always revived and became part of English folklore to the extent that 'eating Dunmow bacon' became a familiar term for a happy married life.

Eating humble pie

The food served at a medieval hunting feast established a marked social distinction between diners. The lord, his family and guests were served venison at high table. Further down the table, those of lesser standing, the huntsmen and retainers, fed on a pie made of the deer's heart, liver and entrails, or 'umbles'.

'Humble pie' is a pun on 'umble pie' and those presented with it are required, metaphorically, to eat inferior food in an inferior position.

Anyone made to 'eat humble pie' is forced to come down from a lofty position they have wrongly assumed, in order to defer to others; frequently those they had previously looked down on.

Going off at half-cock

The hunting field can be hazardous, and in the early days of firearms, it was not the game alone which faced danger from the guns.

Firing an old-fashioned flintlock gun involved releasing a spring-loaded hammer called a 'cock'. Freed by the action of the trigger, this struck a piece of flint against a steel plate, sending sparks into the small charge of powder in the lockpan, which in turn detonated the main charge in the breech of the gun.

When the gun was fully cocked, it could only be discharged by pulling the trigger. 'At half-cock', however, it was liable to go off unexpectedly, often before there had been time to take aim, with the result that the shot was frequently wasted. That is why anything described as 'going off at half-cock' can be taken as premature, ill-prepared and unlikely to succeed.

Going the whole hog

'Going the whole hog' means doing something completely and thoroughly, with no half measures. The saying may well stem from the careful practice in days gone by of using every part of the household pig when it was butchered, to supply meat for the coming winter.

Another interpretation rests on a different meaning of 'hog', which, from the end of the seventeenth century was the slang for a shilling. In this context, 'going the whole hog' means 'spending the whole shilling at once'.

In either case, the saying has an air of determination and resolution that survives today.

Going wool-gathering

During the Middle Ages villagers who were thought to be incapable of other work were set to gather wool torn from sheep by bushes and brambles. Quite apart from the mental state of the wool-gatherers, this necessitated wandering about the fields and hedgerows apparently aimlessly. In time 'going wool-gathering' became a term used of anyone who showed signs of day-dreaming or absent-mindedness.

If beards were all, then goats would preach

This is a more recent version of the older proverb 'An old goat is never the more revered for his beard'. Both carry the meaning that old age alone (identified by the reference to beards) is not a hallmark of wisdom and that true wisdom lies deeper than superficial appearances.

Kicking the bucket

At the beginning of winter it was once common for households to slaughter the pig which they had been fattening through the year. Once killed, the pig's carcass was suspended from a wooden frame, known in the eastern parts of England as a 'bucket', from the French word *buquet* for a beam. Hanging by its heels, it was not uncommon for the carcass to undergo the occasional post-mortem spasm, which made it 'kick the bucket'. From this derived the euphemism for dying which we know today.

Killing the goose which laid the golden egg

The need to balance supply with demand could be a crucial issue in country districts when winter supplies had to be eked out and stocks of seed preserved for the next year's sowing. It was Aesop who enshrined the fable of the goose who laid the golden eggs with proverbial wisdom, but the message it bore has resonated in rural societies ever since.

In Aesop's fable a countryman blessed with a goose which laid golden eggs, thought to make himself even richer by killing the goose, in order to grab all the golden eggs at once. This reckless act, of course, ended the supply of the very eggs he coveted.

Ever since that time, 'killing the goose that laid the golden eggs' has become a metaphor warning against sacrificing future reward and security for immediate gain.

Lamb's wool

Lamb's wool was a traditional country beverage made from the juice of apples roasted in ale, sugar and nutmeg. 'Soft' on the palate, it probably acquired its name from the association of softness with the wool of a lamb.

Locking the stable door after the horse has bolted

Less of a problem than it might once have been, now that cars have replaced horses as the principal mode of transport for many in the countryside and beyond, this proverb is still very much in use (to the extent of featuring in a television advertisement not so long ago).

Its image is graphic and its message stark: taking precautions against a mishap *after* it has happened is a complete waste of time and effort.

Mad as a March hare

March is the month in which hares breed, a time of the year when they indulge in their elaborate and energetic courtship displays. Leaping and running about wildly, the hares appear to be behaving out of character, giving rise to the notion that they are in some way mad.

By association, any individual who behaves abnormally and some-what recklessly might be termed as 'mad as a March hare' too.

Neither fish, flesh nor fowl

Anything described as being 'neither fish, flesh nor fowl' is reckoned to be unsuitable for people of any social standing. The references to three different types of food hark back to the culinary divisions that existed in the Middle Ages: when fish was the food of the clergy, flesh that of the people in general, leaving poultry (fowl) for the very poorest in society.

Anything deemed to be unsuitable for all these groups would not be suitable for anyone (and later anything) at all.

Nest egg

Money laid by acts as an inducement to make further savings, helping the reserve to grow. Referring to this saving as a nest egg alludes to the common practice of placing an egg in a hen's nest to encourage her to lay. The implication in the expression is that even a small sum of money put away stimulates larger savings.

Not until the cows come home

Cattle let out to pasture only come back to the farmyard and the dairy when the next milking is due and even then their return can often be a long-winded process.

From this experience in the fields, 'Not until the cows come home' carries the sense of something taking a very long time indeed, possibly not happening at all, coupled with an air of indolence and procrastination.

Pearls before swine

In St Matthew's gospel, the reference to what became this well known proverb runs:

> *Give not that which is holy unto the dogs, neither cast ye your pearls before swine, lest they trample them under their feet, and turn again and rend you.*

Whether the pearls described are pearls of wisdom or pearls in any other figurative sense, the caution is the same, warning against offering anything of quality to those incapable of appreciating and valuing it.

Pecking order

In the days when hens still roamed freely in farmyards, an order of seniority was established among them, whereby one hen ruled supreme over the rest and could peck any other fowl with impunity. Below her were ranked the rest, finishing with the wretched hen at the bottom, who could be pecked by any of the others. Thus the 'pecking order' was established. Transferred to humans, the 'pecking order' has become an unofficial hierarchy of precedence and superiority that underscores many walks of life.

Pig in a poke

A 'pig in a poke' is a blind bargain, that is to say one entered into without the purchaser knowing for sure what it is that he or she is buying.

The saying dates from the time when live sucking pigs were offered for sale at markets. A common trick played by unscrupulous traders was to display one pig and offer others for sale conveniently tied up in bags.

Only purchasers who had the sense to look inside the bag before handing over their money could be certain of what they were buying. Those who paid first and only checked later could well discover that they had bought a relatively worthless cat or puppy.

And why 'poke'? From the thirteenth century 'poke' was the word for a bag or small sack, derived from the French *poche*, from which we get 'pouch' and 'pocket' in English.

Pigs in clover

The image of 'pigs in clover' is one of unbridled plenty and comfort, a field of succulent clover on which pigs can graze to their hearts' content.

The reference to pigs carries a note of mild disapproval though, when the pigs refer to other people. Here the inference is that some well-fed, in other words well-to-do, people may find themselves leading a life of well-endowed comfort without appreciating how to conduct themselves appropriately.

Putting all your eggs in one basket

This well-known warning may have first appeared in print in a seventeenth-century book of proverbs, but the warning, or something very like, was surely in use long before that.

The allusion is obvious, but the consequences of putting all of the eggs collected in one basket must have been depressingly familiar to anyone who had ever seen the basket dropped and all the eggs smashed.

The caution, quite clearly, is to avoid investing all one has in one speculation or enterprise.

Putting the cart before the horse

'Putting the cart before the horse', so that the animal pushes rather than draws the cart, is a reversal of the natural order that has probably been used as a metaphor for getting things back to front and in the wrong sequence, for as long as horses have been used as draught animals.

The proverb is known in many languages, though in French and Italian oxen are quoted in place of the horse found in the English and German versions.

Red herring

Understanding the origin of this familiar expression is not helped by the fact that only half of it is generally used today.

Most of us accept that a 'red herring' represents anything that is used to divert attention from the principal issue that is being investigated or considered. However, the significance of the saying only becomes clear when we discover that the full wording is 'drawing a red herring across the path'.

The herring in this case was much like a kipper: dried, smoked and salted. Drawn across the path taken by a fox, it would cover the animal's scent and divert pursuing hounds into following a false trail.

Riding a hobby-horse

In time the hobby-horse became widely known as a children's toy made from a stick topped by a horse's head, which the child straddled. However, this was a simplified model of the far more elaborate and much older hobby-horse that first accompanied Morris dancers in their May-Day celebrations to welcome the arrival of spring. These original hobby-horses comprised a light wickerwork frame draped with appropriately decorated cloths.

In either case a hobby-horse became synonymous with something to which an individual was strongly attached. In time this attachment took on an obsessive nature, so that 'riding a hobby-horse' or 'getting on a hobby-horse' came to mean talking at length about a pet project or theory, to the point at which others begin to tire of hearing about it.

Rooks only build nests where there's money

The presence of rooks on a farm was always taken as a sign of good fortune and some farmers even went to the lengths of paying youths to climb trees carrying bags of twigs to build artificial nests in the hope of attracting rooks to settle and bring luck to their farms.

Salt on his tail

It was once believed that if you wanted to catch a bird, you needed to put salt on its tail.

Whatever the truth of this, the idea became well enough established for putting 'salt on his tail' to become a euphemism for apprehending a felon.

Shoeing the goose

Just about the last thing that a goose needs is to have shoes attached to its feet like a horse, and that is the point of this apparently ridiculous notion.

'Shoeing the goose' is an absurd idea, not to mention a complete waste of time. The implication in the saying is the warning that time can be frittered away on trifles rather than concentrating on things which really need to be done.

Similes in truth

This collection of rhyming similes, a good many of which concern animals, was compiled from sayings in use in the Welsh Marches.

As wet as a fish– as dry as a bone.
As live as a bird– as dead as a stone.
As plump as a partridge– as poor as a rat.
As strong as a horse– as weak as a cat.
As hard as a flint– as soft as a mole.
As white as a lily– as black as a coal.
As plain as a pikestaff– as rough as a bear.
As tight as a drum– as free as the air.
As heavy as lead– as light as a feather.
As steady as time– as uncertain as weather.
As hot as an oven– as cold as a frog.
As gay as a lark– as sick as a dog.
As slow as a tortoise– as swift as the wind.
As true as the gospel– as false as mankind.
As thin as a herring– as fat as a pig.
As proud as a peacock– as blithe as a grig.
As savage as tigers– as mild as a dove.
As stiff as a poker– as limp as a glove.
As blind as a bat– as deaf as a post.
As cool as a cucumber– as warm as toast.
As flat as a flounder– as round as a ball.
As blunt as a hammer– as sharp as an awl.
As red as a ferret– as safe as the stocks.

As bold as a thief— as sly as a fox.
As grey as a badger— as green as a parrot.
As long as my arm— as short as a carrot.
As tame as a rabbit— as wild as a hare.
As sound as an acorn— as decayed as a pear.
As busy as ants— as nimble as goats.
As silly as geese— as stinking as stoats.
As fresh as a daisy— as sweet as a nut.
As bright as a ruby— as bitter as soot.
As straight as an arrow— as crooked as a bow.
As yellow as saffron— as black as a sloe.
As brittle as glass— as tough as gristle.
As neat as my nail— as clean as a whistle.
As good as a feast— as bad as a witch.
As light as the day— as dark as pitch.
As wide as a river— as deep as a well.
As still as a mouse— as sound as a bell.
As sure as a gun— as true as a clock.
As frail as a promise— as true as a rock.
As brisk as a bee— as dull as an ass.
As full as a tick— as solid as brass.
As lean as a greyhound— as rich as a Jew.
And ten thousand similes equally true.

Spare at the spigot and spoil at the bung

A 'spigot' is a small peg which is inserted into the vent hole of a barrel or cask, the allusion here being to one filled with a valuable liquid such as beer or wine.

As a metaphor, this saying points to the owner's meanness over small things, shown by his care not to waste any of the barrel's valuable contents at the vent hole, while overlooking the main bung sealing the barrel, through which his drink is leaking in profusion.

To 'spare at the spigot and spoil at the bung' therefore, means to be tight-fisted about things that don't matter, while being wasteful when it comes to those which really are important.

Stalking horse

Horses were not always used in the hunt to pursue game. At one time hunters were accustomed to dismount and hide behind their mounts, which moved steadily towards the quarry until the hunters were within aim. In time actual horses were replaced by artificial horses that amounted to a hide-cum-decoy.

The sense of concealment used to gain closer access to a goal, was taken up in the political arena during the nineteenth century, when a 'stalking horse' became a candidate who was put forward in an election to test the water for another and, potentially, far more successful candidate.

In British politics a 'stalking horse' has been used to challenge for the leadership of political parties. The candidate in question has had no realistic chance of winning the election. His role has been to gauge the weight of support for a challenge to the current leader and to reveal how well stronger candidates might fare in a leadership contest.

Straight from the horse's mouth

The only sure way of establishing the age of a horse is to examine its front teeth. This provided incontrovertible proof, so much so that 'straight from the horse's mouth' became synonymous with the most senior and highly respected source on any given subject.

Tarred with the same brush

The metaphorical action of 'tarring with the same brush', is to condemn someone, or a group of people, for the same reason that you condemn others, whether that condemnation is justified or not.

The saying stems from the use of tar by shepherds in earlier times. Cuts and other sores on the skin of sheep used to be treated by a dab with a brush dipped in tar. Once all the sheep had been treated, all had been 'tarred with the same brush', in other words they had all been treated in the same way without distinction or discrimination.

Wild goose chase

Today we use the saying 'wild goose chase' in the sense of a vain pursuit. But the original meaning of 'wild goose chase' dates from a time when a game of follow-my-leader on horseback was popular in rural England. It was called a 'wild goose chase' because the appearance of the riders, evenly spaced one behind the other, resembled the formation of wild geese in flight. In this usage a 'wild goose chase' figuratively represented a rapidly changing course of events which involved quick wits to stay in touch with what was happening.

By the middle of the eighteenth century the modern meaning had replaced the earlier one and a 'wild goose chase' became an absurd enterprise; an impracticable or useless pursuit of an unachievable goal.

You can take a horse to (the) water but you cannot make him drink

This saying has been recorded in English, in various forms with and without 'the', from the twelfth century.

The inference is clear: there is always a point at which an obstinate or determined individual will refuse to be drawn in a desired direction, no matter how beneficial that may be.

touching
wood

There were sayings and superstitions about good and bad luck in almost every aspect of country life in days gone by, of which a fair number have passed into common usage today.

'Touching wood' is a good example of a superstition that has become a well-rooted phrase, even if its origins are now obscured and largely forgotten.

Some people reckon that saying 'touch wood' is sufficient to safeguard against bad luck; though physically touching a piece of wood will only satisfy the truly superstitious.

In the Christian tradition the 'wood' to be touched is generally associated with the wooden cross on which Jesus Christ was crucified. However, the wood from certain trees has been endowed with special powers since ancient times. It was once widely believed that the elder tree, for example, had the power of protecting those carrying it from spells cast by witches and wizards. The same was held to be true of wood from the roan, or witch elm.

From the benefits associated with 'An apple a day keeps the doctor away' to a wish made to a distant star, country sayings and the superstitions associated with them have carried the hopes and fears of generations – as many still do today.

An apple a day keeps the doctor away

This well-known piece of dietary advice may be an early forerunner of the current belief among dieticians that our health improves when we eat five portions of fresh fruit and vegetables every day.

In 1866 a proverb quoted in *Notes & Queries* ran:

Eat an apple on going to bed,
And you'll keep the doctor from earning his bread.

A rose by any other name

Around the country common flowers have acquired a variety of local names according to related superstitions, of which these are a few:

Marsh-marigolds became known as 'drunkards', from the belief that picking them or even looking at them intently would turn you to drink.

Poppies became known as 'ear-aches' because, if they were gathered and placed close to the ear, they would bring on a violent ear-ache.

In the North of England poppies were also thought to damage the eyes to the point of causing blindness if they were held too close; this gave rise to the country name of 'blindy-buff'.

A speck of gifts

A white speck on a finger nail became known around the country as a 'gift' and, depending on which finger nail it was on, a 'gift' was thought to foretell events, as follows:

A gift on the thumb indicates a present;
A gift on the forefinger a friend or lover;
A gift on the middle finger a foe;
A gift on the fourth finger a visit to pay;
A gift on the little finger a journey to go.

Ash leaves for luck

In the southern counties of England girls used ash leaves to determine who they would marry.

First an ash leaf was plucked from a branch and put in the left hand while these lines were recited:

The even ash leaf in my hand,
The first I meet shall be my man.

Then the ash leaf was put in a glove with the lines:

The even ash leaf in my glove,
The first I meet shall be my love.

Finally the leaf was tucked into the girl's bosom as she repeated:

The even ash leaf in my bosom,
The first I meet shall be my husband.

Birthday greetings

This rhyme, popular with children from generations back, reminds us that the day of the week on which we were born was traditionally believed to have particular significance:

Monday's child is fair of face,
Tuesday's child is full of grace,
Wednesday's child is full of woe,
Thursday's child has far to go,
Friday's child is loving and giving,
Saturday's child works hard for a living,
But the child that is born on the Sabbath Day
Is blithe and bonny, good and gay.

Bless you!

Sneezing on different days of the week was once believed to have a bearing on your future, according to this much-quoted saying:

Sneeze on a Monday, you sneeze for danger;
Sneeze on a Tuesday, you kiss a stranger;
Sneeze on a Wednesday, you sneeze for a letter;
Sneeze on a Thursday, for something better;
Sneeze on a Friday, you sneeze for sorrow;
Sneeze on a Saturday, your sweetheart tomorrow;
Sneeze on a Sunday, your safety seek,
The Devil will have you the whole of the week.

Blessings from birds

One old rhyme singles out these four birds for special recognition, ensuring that their nests were always respected and never robbed of their eggs:

The robin and the wren,
Are God Almighty's cock and hen.
The swallow and the swift,
Are God Almighty's gifts.

As a consequence of this it was always held to be lucky to have swallows or martins nesting under your eaves.

Charm for burns

In addition to applying soothing lotions made from elder and butter, or the creamy juice of house-leeks, it was customary in parts of the country to recite a charm as well, along the lines of:

> *Three Angels came from North, East and West,*
> *One brought fire, another brought frost,*
> *And the third brought the Holy Ghost.*
> *So out fire and in frost.*
> *In the name of the Father, Son and Holy Ghost.*

Cream of the well

It was once the custom in farming communities for servants to sit up to see in the New Year and, at midnight, to rush for the 'cream of the well': the first water drawn from the well in the year. This was thought to be beautifying and lucky and the maid who succeeded in drawing it would be rewarded by her mistress, who symbolically bought it from her maid with the gift of a coin when it was brought to her room.

Cure for warts

In central parts of England removing warts used to involve an ash tree and a new pin.

People wishing to rid themselves of warts would go to an ash tree and there carefully prick each wart with the new pin, before driving it into the tree's bark while reciting the words:

Ashen tree, ashen tree,
Pray buy these warts of me.

Curing thorn pricks

Anyone cut by the prick of a thorn had this charm at hand to speed its healing:

Christ was of a virgin born,
And he was pricked by a thorn,
And it did never bell [fester] nor swell,
As I trust in Jesus this never will.

Cutting nails

By tradition people were supposed to cut their nails on a Monday in preference to any other day of the week. Sunday was the least propitious day to do it, because that was the day when the Devil cut his nails, and this old rhyme extends the warning to cutting hair as well as nails ('horn'):

He that on the Sabbath morn
Cutteth either hair or horn
Will rue the day that he was born.

Another version offers this advice:

Cut nails on Monday, cut them for health
Cut them on Tuesday, cut them for wealth
Cut them on Wednesday, cut them for news
Cut them on Thursday, a pair of new shoes
Cut them on Friday, cut them for sorrow
Cut them on Saturday, see your true love tomorrow
But cut them on Sunday, your safety seek
For Old Nick'll have you, the rest of the week.

Dimples

The position of dimples was once thought to have some bearing on your future prosperity:

A dimple in your cheek,
Your living to seek;
A dimple in your chin,
You'll have your living brought in.

Fiery tempers

In the days when country houses still had maids, it was not uncommon to hear one who was having difficulty lighting a fire complaining:

Oh dear, my young man's in a temper.

Flowers out of season

Flowers out of season
Trouble without reason.

Any interruption to the orderly rhythm of nature has always been taken as a portent of uncertain times ahead and the blooming of flowers out of season was once seen by many country dwellers as foretelling death or disaster.

Even more alarming was a second, autumnal, blooming of a fruit tree, especially if fruit and blossom appeared together:

A bloom on the tree when the apples are ripe,
Is a sure termination of somebody's life.

In the middle of the nineteenth century a Welsh correspondent in *Notes & Queries* shared this thought-provoking encounter with fellow readers:

Last year I was walking in the garden of a neighbouring farmer, aged seventy-one. We came up to an apple-tree, heavily laden with nearly ripe fruit, and perceived a sprig of very late bloom, a kind of second edition. He told me rather gravely, that in his boyhood this occurrence was invariably held to herald a death in the family in two or three months' time. On my joking him about Welsh credulity, he pretended not to believe the idle lore, but was evidently glad to pass from the subject. His brother, aged sixty-eight, in perfect health then, who resided in the same house, was dead within six weeks! A few weeks afterwards walking in our own orchard, I discovered a still later blossom on a Ribstone Pippin tree, and called a man-servant, aged sixty-three, to look at it. He at once told me, with some concern, that it always foretold death in the family; he had known many instances. Singularly enough, he himself was dead in a very few weeks.

Hair of the dog

An old folk remedy for healing a wound caused by a dog bite, was to place a burnt hair from the dog which had given the bite on the wound. Unlikely as it may seem, this was believed to be the best cure for dog bites.

From this has come the metaphorical use of the term 'hair of the dog' to describe an old cure for a hangover, which consists of drinking the following morning a little of the same beverage that had brought on the hangover in the first place.

So, 'hair of the dog' is often the rueful comment made by the sufferer of a hangover at the first taste of drink the following day.

Handle with care

Hand tools once used in the field and the gardening tools of today come with long-established superstitions. According to one ominous saying:

For if in your house a man shoulders a spade,
For you and your kinsfolk a grave is half made.

Sharp tools accidentally carried into a house should be removed through the same doorway to prevent them 'cutting' the household's good fortune.

There are risks attached to leaving a rake lying on the ground with the teeth pointing upwards, and the risk is not restricted to the feet of anyone treading on the rake by accident. Superstition holds that bad luck will follow, either in the form of a poor crop or unwanted rain.

Hawthorn bloom and elder flowers

Hawthorn bloom and elder flowers
Fill the house with evil powers.

This prejudice against taking hawthorn blossom into a house extends to fruit bloom as well: apple, plum and pear blossom are similarly blighted by the risk of bringing bad luck into a house.

The danger posed by elder flowers is the apparent attraction they hold for snakes. Adders have been known to shelter in the roots of elder and the smell of creamy elder flowers is said to attract snakes.

Holly trees round the house prevent sorcery

'Holly cottages' are found throughout the English countryside accounting for the widespread belief that holly is a powerful ally in keeping evil spirits at bay.

In this the holly is helped by its good name and by its prickly leaves and bright red berries, which were believed to be especially abhorrent to witches, which explains why many hollies stand as guardians in hedges and gardens, preserving the houses they protect from one generation to the next.

Holly trees are free from the threat of damage by animals and a holly that grows through self-seeding brings even greater good fortune to the owner whose land it has chosen to grow on.

Jumping over the broomstick

'Jumping over the broomstick' has become a euphemism for a marriage that takes place quite informally without significant preparation or ceremony.

It is a curious saying which owes its origin to unconventional practice, observed among itinerant country groups especially, of establishing 'married status' through the happy couple's ceremonial jumping over a broomstick; or 'jumping over a besom' to quote an alternative form.

Keeping the watch on St Mark's Eve

The eve of St Mark (25 April) was one of the dates in the calendar when future husbands could be divined. This involved staying awake until midnight, though with careful application the results were presumably worth the effort.

On St Mark's Eve, at twelve o'clock,
The fair maid will watch her smock,
To find her husband in the dark,
By praying unto good St Mark.

Knotting the garter

Tying three knots in the left garter was another time-honoured way in which girls wishing to marry might catch a glimpse of their future husbands and determine their feelings towards them, as this rhyme illustrates:

This knot, this knot, this knot I knit,
To see the thing I ne'er saw yet –
To see my love in his array,
And what he walks in every day;
And what his occupation be,
This night I in my sleep may see.

And if my love be clad in green,
His love for me is surely seen;
And if my love is clad in grey,

His love for me is far away;
But if my love be clad in blue,
His love for me is very true.

Luck of spilling

Not all spilling was an evil omen that required placating the devil. Many country people firmly believed the old adage:

Spill salt for sorrow,
Spill sugar for joy.

Lucky bits and lucky bones

At one time great faith was placed in talismans to ward off danger and to increase prosperity.

The dried tip of a calf's tongue was reckoned to be especially propitious. Carried in a pocket, it became known as a 'lucky-bit', to guard against danger and to ensure that the pocket in which it was kept was never without money.

Money was also the principal objective in carrying a so-called 'lucky-bone', or coracoid bone of a chicken or other farmyard fowl. Placed in a pocket or purse, it too was meant to encourage a ready supply of money.

Need-fire

The 'need-fire' was one of the principal charms against cattle diseases in days gone by. It comprised a virgin flame kindled by the friction of two pieces of wood. Carried hastily from village to village, it was used to protect cattle from infection.

Writing of the Coronation Bonfires in June 1911, a correspondent in *The Times* observed:

These 'need-fires' have continued in the north of England within living memory. The writer has spoken with farmers in Cumberland and Westmorland who in a time of cattle plague have not only seen the 'need-fire' carried from farm to farm, but cattle driven through the smoke to stop the murrain.

The belief in the 'need-fire' has ensured its survival in popular memory through a number of sayings. 'To be at a thing like need-fire', means to undertake it with great effort and industry. 'To go like need-fire' means to go at great speed. And 'To work for need-fire' implies working with great effort or restless activity.

New Year pennies

Children in search of pennies used to sing this song for their would-be benefactors:

I wish you a merry Christmas
And a happy New Year,

A pocket full of money,
And a cellar full of beer;
A good fat pig
That will last you all year;
I wish you a merry Christmas
And a happy New Year.

The cock flew up in the yew tree,
The hen came chuckling by;
If you haven't got any money,
Please to give me a mince pie –
A mince pie this New Year.

The roads are very dirty,
My shoes are very thin,
I've got a little pocket
I can pop a penny in.
May God bless all friends dear.

I wish you a merry Christmas,
And a happy New Year.
A lump of cake
And a barrel of beer.
Christmas comes but once a year;
When it comes it brings good cheer.
Cheer up, cheer up, this New Year.

Nuts and babies

Hazelnuts used to be offered to brides to assist with the creation of a family and a year in which there was a good crop of nuts was widely held to be a good one for babies as well:

Plenty of nuts, plenty of cradles.

goes the saying.

Paring apples

Paring an apple in the hope that the thrown skin may reveal the initial of a future spouse was once a very popular form of marital divination. John Gay, in *The Shepherd's Week* wrote:

I pare this pippin round and round again,
My shepherd's name to flourish on the plain.
I fling th'unbroken paring o'er my head,
Upon the grass a perfect L is read.

Pins and luck

There is contradictory advice about the wisdom of picking up pins you find lying about. Presumably this leaves you free to interpret your fate as you wish, either by leaving the pins where they are or picking them up.

Pick up pins, pick up sorrow.

warns one saying. While the other advises:

See a pin and pick it up,
All the day you'll have good luck.

This is supported by a further rhyme:

See a pin and let it lie,
You'll want a pin before you die.

Rearing babies

Achieving the right temperature balance for babies was seen as having a significant impact on their later life in days gone by. One old country saying advised the following:

Keep the feet warm and the head cold,
They'll live to grow old.

St Faith and future husbands

It was once a custom in the north of England for future husbands to be divined on St Faith's Day (6 October) by means of a specially prepared cake.

The author of *Observations on the Popular Antiquities of Great Britain*, described the typical observances paid on St Faith's Day as they were practised in the first half of the nineteenth century:

A cake of flour, spring water, salt and sugar must be made by three maidens or widows, and each must have an equal share in the composition. It is baked in a Dutch oven, in silence, and the cake must be turned nine times, or three times to each person. When it is baked it is divided into three parts. Each cook takes her share, dividing it into nine slips; each slip must be passed three times through a wedding ring borrowed from a woman who has been married at least seven years. Then each maid or widow must eat her nine slips, repeating the following rhyme:

O good St Faith, be kind tonight,
And bring to me my heart's delight;
Let me my future husband view,
And be my visions chaste and true.

All three get into bed with the ring suspended by a string to the head of the couch; they will be sure to dream of their future husbands.

Salt and sorrow

Help me to salt, help me to sorrow.

is an old saying, dating from the time when salt was an essential commodity for preserving food.

In some traditional farming families it was still common until well into the nineteenth century for there to be one large salt-cellar on the table; the master and his family sat above the salt, the maidservants and male farm servants below the salt.

Secret of a blush

There is more than a hint of selfishness in this old country charm, but the secret of the blush is something very private indeed:

Right cheek, left cheek, why do you burn?
Cursed be she that doth me any harm.

If it be a maid, let her be slayed,
If it be a wife, let her lose her life,
And if it be a widow, long let her mourn;
But if it be my own true love, burn, cheek, burn.

Sowing hempseed

Hempseed I set, hempseed I sow,
The man that is my true love,
Come after and mow.

This was the old rhyme which girls were meant to recite as they walked through a garden or churchyard on Midsummer Eve (23 June), throwing hempseed over their shoulder.

This was supposed to summon the phantom of a future husband, mowing or raking into a winding sheet behind her.

A variation of this requires the girl to go backwards into a garden at midnight on Midsummer Eve, where she then made her way backwards around it, scattering hempseed with her right hand while intoning:

Hempseed I sow;
Hempseed is to grow;
And the man that my husband is to be,
Let him follow after and mow.

If all went well, a vision of her husband, scythe in hand, would duly appear.

T for two

One of the less demanding ways of divining the image of a future husband was to summon up a dream of him on Midsummer Eve. This involved carefully arranging one's shoe at the bedside, while reciting the rhyme:

Hoping this night my true love to see,
I place my shoes in the form of a T.

Shoes could also be crossed on a Friday night, while intoning:

I put my left shoe over my right
In hopes this night I may see
The man that shall my husband be
In his apparel and in his array
And in the clothes he wears every day;
What he does and what he wears
And what he'll do all days and years,
Whether I sleep or whether I wake
I hope to hear my true love speak.

Telling the bees

At one time it was common practice throughout the country to tell the bees of a household when the master, or some other member of the family, had died. If the bees were not formally told, it was believed that they would either fly away never to return, or would all die themselves.

In some parts of the country the bees were informed of the death as the funeral procession left the house for the church, though in other areas it was customary to tell them in the middle of the night.

The form of words used varied as well, but whatever was said, it was whispered to the bees in their hive with great solemnity. Variations of how to 'tell the bees' included:

The master is dead.

Your friend's gone.

The poor master's dead, but you must work for me.

Bees, bees, bees, your master is dead, and you must work for [the name of the future owner].

Toasts for harvests and other festivals

Feasting was an important part of country life, providing an opportunity for the community on a farm to join together to celebrate mutual success and extend greetings and hopes for mutual prosperity. These frequently took the form of traditional toasts. Here are a few examples:

Here's to the champion, of the white horn,
Here's God send the master a good crop of corn;
Of wheat, rye, and barley, and all sorts of grain,
If we live to this time twelvemonth we'll drink his health again.

Good health to the master, and all on his farm;
May he live long and prosper, and grow good crops of corn;
Wheat, oats, beans and barley, yea, and all kinds of grain,
So that he may have plenty, to treat us again.

Here behold and see my glass full,
I'll take 'em off at such a pull;
I'll take 'em off as you shall find,
I scarce shall leave one drop behind.
Here's a health to you my brother, Tom,
It's time that you and I were gone,
We'll drink and stand our ground . . .
And that is called the Ploughboy's round.

Here's to the rose that's in full bloom.
And I hope it'll never be blighted;
Here's to the young man that's constant and true,
And I hope he'll never be slighted.

Long may you live,
Happy may you be,
Blest with content,
And from misfortunes free.

Valentine preparations

St Valentine's Day (14 February) was an important date in the calendar for those wishing to cement a love pact with their intended. Careful preparations had to be made the night before, leading to the day itself when successful girls would look upon the first man they saw, who was destined to become their husband:

Thee first I spied, and the first swain we see
In spite of fortune shall our true-love be.

The detailed lengths to which some would-be-brides went are illustrated in this account of preparations made by the young writer on St Valentine's Eve well over a century ago:

Last Friday was Valentine's Day, and the night before I got five bay leaves, and pinned four of them to the four corners of my pillow, and the fifth to the middle; and then, if I dreamt of my sweetheart, Betty said we should be married before the year was out. But, to make it more sure, I boiled an egg hard and took out the yolk and filled it with salt; and, when I went to bed, ate it shell and all without speaking or drinking after it. We also wrote our lovers' names upon bits of paper, and rolled them up in clay and put them into water; and the first that rose up was to be our Valentine. Would you think it, Mr Blossom was my man? I lay a-bed and shut my eyes all the morning till he came to our house; for I would not have seen another man before him for all the world.

Washing blankets

Surprising as it may seem, May, the month when spring really becomes established, is dogged with more than its share of superstition. For instance, in several parts of the country women never dreamt of washing blankets in May, for the simple reason that:

Wash blankets in May,
You'll soon be under clay.

Wedding colours

Brides did not always wear white on their wedding days and the colours they chose were believed to indicate much about what lay in store for them in the years ahead:

Married in white, you have chosen right
Married in grey, you will go far away
Married in black, you will wish yourself back
Married in red, you will wish yourself dead
Married in green, ashamed to be seen
Married in blue, you will always be true
Married in pearl, you will live in a whirl
Married in yellow, ashamed of your fellow
Married in brown, you will live out of town
Married in pink, your fortune will sink.

Wedding day warnings

The choice of wedding day has carried considerable significance for many generations.

May has not always been regarded as a propitious month, as these variations of the well known saying state:

Marry in May, rue for aye.

and, even bleaker:

Marry in May
And you'll rue the day
And wed povertaie.

It was generally advised to avoid marrying in Lent as well, on the grounds that:

Marry in Lent, live to repent.

The day of the week was portentous too:

Monday for wealth,
Tuesday for health,
Wednesday best of all,
Thursday for losses,
Friday for crosses
And Saturday no luck at all.

Wishes in the stars

The first star seen in the night sky held particular promise to believers in the old saying:

Star light, star bright,
The first star I've seen tonight.
Would it were that I might
Have the wish I wish tonight.

Witches and rowan

Of all plants and trees, the rowan tree, or mountain ash, was regarded as being the most protective against witches.

Twigs from a rowan tree were placed over cottage and farmhouse doorways; they were fastened to cattle stalls; and cowherds and carters had whipstocks made from rowan wood as well, for without its protection a witch was thought to be perfectly capable of bringing a draught team to a standstill:

Woe to the lad
Without a rowan-tree gad.

and:

If you whipstock's made of rown.
You may ride through any town.